TAYLOR
—ON HOCKEY—

TAYLOR
—ON HOCKEY—

Ian Taylor
with David Vear

Macdonald
Queen Anne Press

A *Queen Anne Press* BOOK

© Ian Taylor and David Vear 1988

First published in Great Britain in 1988 by
Queen Anne Press, a division of
Macdonald & Co (Publishers) Ltd
3rd Floor
Greater London House
Hampstead Road
London
NW1 7QX

A member of Maxwell Pergamon Publishing Corporation plc

Jacket photographs – Front: Ian Taylor playing for England v Pakistan,
World Cup 1986 (Colorsport)
Back: Ian Taylor with Player of the Year Trophy,
1986 (Colorsport)

Line drawings by Mei Lim

British Library Cataloguing in Publication Data

Taylor, Ian
  Taylor on hockey.
  1. Field hockey
  I. Title II. Vear, David
  796.35'5   GV1017.H7

  ISBN 0-356-15140-9

Typeset by Hazell Watson and Viney Ltd, Aylesbury,
and Fullpoint Filmsetting Ltd, London.
Printed & bound in Great Britain by
PURNELL BOOK PRODUCTION LIMITED
A MEMBER OF BPCC plc

Picture credits

Allsport 60 (Simon Bruty), 65 (Bob Martin), 66 (Simon Bruty) ; Coloursport 72,
78, 79; Peter Luck 14, 18, 19, 24, 26, 34, 43, 47, 57, 63, 64, 68, 69, 70 *top,* 80,
86, 87, 89, 127; Morley Pecker 37, 52, 55, 59, 70 *bottom,* 71, 94, 100, 110, 112; Pat
Rowley 39 (Francotte), 54 (Jeroen van Bergen), 75 (Richard Oliver/Select), 101
(Dieter Rombardt); Slazenger Hockey 83.

Contents

Introduction   7
The Dribble   11
The Push   22
Stopping the Ball   27
The Hit   38
The Flick   46
Beating an Opponent   51
Tackling   56
Goalscoring   73
Goalkeeping   81
Team and Group Play   95
Systems and Set Pieces   102
Coaching and Training   114
Hockey Records   128

INTRODUCTION

International hockey is a fast, furious game of remarkable complexity, and the variety of skills displayed can bemuse even the most knowledgeable spectator. At the highest level these movements are the result of years of painstaking practice by players who've made many sacrifices in the interests of the sport to reach the game's premier stage. However, one of the truly great things about the game is the fact that it can be enjoyed by almost everyone with an interest in sporting activity.

Hockey at any level is a thrilling game enjoyed by players of all ages. The vast majority play the game primarily for social reasons and do not normally have the opportunity for the sort of coaching that could significantly improve both their individual skills and overall performance. In truth, improvements in technique and fitness can only enhance one's enjoyment of the game so everyone should take the opportunity to learn a little more of what it is all about.

Within the pages of this book, I will be taking you through the mechanics of even the most complex individual moves, using some of the finest players in the world game as my examples. The basics you will use in every game; other skills will need a lot of practice before you will want to risk using them in full match conditions. With the extensive use of photographs and diagrams I hope to help players to spot weaknesses in their game, and help coaches to pinpoint faults among members of their teams.

Having said all that, the overall aim of the book is to help everyone gain more satisfaction from this wonderful game and, if possible, persuade those of you who may have thought about taking up the challenge to finally summon up the courage to leave your armchair and go out and play. Hockey has always been a popular sport at school level but, too often, promising young players drift away from the game once they leave school because they never think of finding and joining a local club. With interest in the sport at an unprecedented level, many clubs are now expanding in such a way that they can offer teams over a wide range of playing standards. What is more, unlike soccer, where most players tend to hang up their boots sometime in their early thirties, hockey teams can embrace several age groups with youth players in their early teens learning their skills from the older hands whose depth of experience makes up more than adequately for the slowing down of their legs. In an encouraging attempt to 'catch 'em young', many clubs are now actively promoting their family image by encouraging parents to bring their children along with them at weekends and allow them to have some fun with a stick and ball. This way, youngsters who demonstrate an appetite for the game can learn the basics at their own pace, ready for their first taste of organised hockey some time around their seventh birthday.

The emergence of the artificial playing surface as the international standard for hockey has done much to make a book such as this worthwhile. Artificial turf has revolutionised the sport and inspired a whole range of new techniques which would be near impossible to perform on conventional grass pitches. Season by season, more and more players of all standards are gaining access to artificial turf and so it follows that the scope for the improvement of individual skills has broadened.

It is not only the quality of the playing surface that has improved immeasurably in recent years. Equipment has undergone a revolution too and it is now possible to find a range of first class gear to suit any pocket. Again I hope to be able to offer useful advice to both players and coaches.

Because I want this book to have as broad an appeal as possible, I have deliberately chosen to steer clear of some of the complexities of team play and the disciplines of set-pieces. My target is the individual and the contribution he or she can make in the overall performance of the team. However, I do intend to introduce the basics of system play and include some examples of the more significant ploys I have seen developed in recent years, along with some explanation of the advantages and disadvantages as I see them. This chapter will also cover the role of the coach in combining and synchronising a group of proficient individuals into a successful team.

The skills and moves that will be demonstrated within these pages are the work of some of the top players in the modern game. I have particularly chosen my own contemporaries because they are the best qualified to demonstrate skills that would have been beyond comprehension on the muddy, bumpy, grass pitches of ten years ago.

Let me stress that this is by no means a book to be looked at and then put away on the shelf and forgotten about. Each particular skill has been broken down and analysed in words, pictures and drawings with the intention of helping the reader to 'copy' it and in doing so improve their individual game. I hope it will be taken out onto the practice field and consulted in the club bar after the game. I want the coach to keep it in his locker and the player in his kit-bag.

Finally I should stress that although it has been written by a man, this book is intended to apply equally to both the men's and women's game. After years of resistance, the women's game has finally taken on its own truly competitive edge. The laws governing both men's and women's hockey are now virtually the same and either sex is capable of perfecting the skills I'll be discussing.

If, at the end of the day, players of all standards improve their own skills to some degree and go on to gain more satisfaction and enjoyment from their game, I will be happy to have achieved what I set out to do.

Ian. C.B. Taylor.
England & Great Britain.

THE DRIBBLE

Of all the basic skills in hockey, the dribble is the one which can most often open up a game and create that all important goal-scoring chance. It seems logical, therefore, that an instructional book of this nature should start with this vital aspect of play. What is more, the dribble is one of the easiest skills to practise because it can be performed in a confined space – in the garden, the front drive or even the sitting room, assuming everyone else in the house is of a tolerant disposition.

Before I can begin demonstrating the art of the dribble, or indeed any of the passing skills for that matter, it is important firstly to stress the need to adopt the right style of grip on the stick itself. Nowadays, it is commonly accepted that the stick can be held equally effectively in a number of ways, but at the same time I should point out that each modification is really only a minor improvisation on the basic technique. Broadly speaking, those who have experimented suc-cessfully have been experienced players looking to introduce that extra 'special' ingredient to their game and enable them to out-smart their opponents at the highest level. For the beginner – as with most sports – there is a basic right and wrong way to pick up the hockey stick and this technique should be perfected before any thoughts of refinement are entertained.

The stick must be held in a way that enables some movement of the hands. As you progress further into this book, you will realise just how important this movement is when tackling some of the more complex skills in the game.

To obtain the best grip, start by laying the stick on the ground with its face towards the playing surface. The thumb and forefinger are then spread to produce a 'V' shape (see fig. 1), with the left hand grasping the upper end and the right positioned a comfortable distance (15–30 cm) lower down. The 'V' of the left hand should be pointing directly down the back of the stick. Once accom-

Fig. 1 *The basic grips: Once the stick has been grasped from the floor, with the V-shape of both hands facing down the back of the stick, a small rotational movement of the hands will create slight strengths and weaknesses in different strokes. The 'English' grip (a) allows more freedom of movement in the pushing and flicking strokes, while the 'Bradman-style' grip (b) eliminates the weaknesses on the reverse side often associated with the English grip. Faults in the basic grip are the cause of many of the average player's weaknesses, and the grip should always be an area for close attention, particularly when examining weaknesses on the reverse side. Once the basic grip has been mastered it can be adapted and modified to individual tastes.*

plished you will have formed the conventional grip. Naturally there will be some movement of these positions when executing particular manoeuvres, such as hitting the ball for example, but for dribbling, pushing and flicking, this grip will be the most suitable.

Try to keep any movement of the top hand to a minimum. You should particularly avoid allowing the hand to slide around the top of the stick because if you allow such a fault to develop at this stage you will find it more difficult to effectively execute some of the later skills. If, for instance, you allow your top (left) hand to slip around towards the face of the stick, you will be creating a potential weakness for the future when you come to learn how to trap the ball. This problem will be particularly apparent when performing the manoeuvre on the reverse side.

The conventional grip may seem uncomfortable at first and there may be a natural tendency to modify straight away. Indeed, one only has to observe the technique of England and Great Britain centre-forward Sean Kerly, one of the most gifted players in the game today, to see that the unconventional grip – even though in real terms it only amounts to a movement of about half a centimetre around the stick – has become an integral and highly successful part of his game. However, it should be pointed out that Sean, in common with all of us, did get his basics right first of all. His improvisation is based on years of experience – a conscious move to adopt a slightly unorthodox grip to create the flair that has lifted him up among the greats of recent years.

So remember: get the basic grip sorted out in the beginning. Most players taking up the game will find techniques far easier if they start by positioning the right hand low down the stick. Because it is the left hand that will be doing most of the moving during the course of any game, it follows that by keeping the opening position as low as possible you will be giving yourself the maximum flexibility when it comes to executing some of the more difficult skills I will be describing later. Left hand strength and manipulation is vital, so much so that the left-handed player has a distinct advantage over a right-handed opponent.

Take all the time you need to get this aspect of your game sorted out right from the beginning because it will almost certainly govern your development as you move forward towards more advanced techniques. Work hard until you feel yourself comfortable with the basics – there will be plenty of opportunities to experiment once you have mastered the fundamentals of the game or sorted out those flaws that may have been hampering your progress so far. Once you're happy with these basics, it's time to start practising the dribble.

The Open-sided Dribble

Throughout the open-sided dribble, the ball should remain in constant contact with the stick. The stick itself should be held just outside the line of the right foot on the forestick side and with the ball running just in front of the body. To carry out this movement correctly the body will need to be slightly crouched while running. At first, practising this skill can prove uncomfortable because the back and upper hamstring will be taking most of the strain.

Start practising the exercise slowly and then gradually increase your momentum. Once you begin running more quickly, you will find that the natural momentum of the ball will push it a little further in front of the body. This will exaggerate the crouching effect still further. Remember also that even the most breathtaking dribble from one of the world's leading exponents of the skill will last only seconds – and by the time you reach that standard your body will have well and truly adapted to the stance!

For the dribble, the left (upper) hand controls the angle of the face of the stick while the right maintains contact between the stick and the ball. You are now dribbling with the open face, and, by varying the speed of your running and ensuring that the ball is kept under constant control, you can begin creating problems for your opponent. Simply by carrying the ball beyond your opponent and then accelerating, it is possible to leave him or her completely stranded. Executed properly, this can be one of the most exciting movements in modern hockey. The great former Pakistani captains Kaleemulah and Samiullah were two of the finest demonstrators of this particular skill, and would use an electrifying change of pace to devastating effect, appearing to carry the ball past their opponents with consummate ease. Thomas Rek of West Germany is now emulating their style.

The dribble: Stephen Batchelor of England and Great Britain demonstrates the perfect position while dribbling the ball past the New Zealand defender in the 1986 World Cup. With back and knees bent and the stick and ball in constant contact, he accelerates beyond the defender. This most straightforward of dribbling skills, when performed with skill and speed, can devastate a defence simply by carrying the ball beyond an opponent.

The key points to remember for the open-sided dribble, then, are these:

- Work hard to feel comfortable with the correct grip, and position the hands slightly apart (fig. 1);

- Run with the ball and stick outside the line of the right foot;

- Always keep the ball in front of you;

- Make sure your knees and back are slightly crouched.

The Stop Dribble

Once you feel comfortable with the open-sided dribble and are happy that your grip is correct, we can begin looking at some variations – after all, your game would quickly become limited if you could do nothing with the ball other than run it in a straight line!

It is essential to understand right from the beginning that all movement of the stick, when the intention is to keep its face in contact with the ball, is controlled by the left (top) hand. However, it soon becomes obvious that, unless the right hand relaxes its grip from time to time, both forearms will quickly become hopelessly tangled. Looking at the example below (fig. 2), you will see that the left

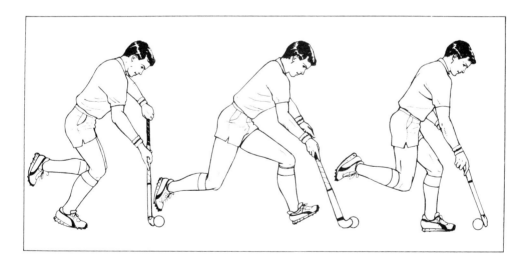

Fig. 2 *The stop dribble: To slow down the pace of the ball, or to change direction, the ball can be controlled or stopped by turning the stick over the top of the ball using the left hand in an anti-clockwise direction (as though turning a door knob). The right hand simply lets the stick rotate within it, grasping and supporting at the extremities of each movement. For this and the other dribbling skills to develop smoothly, it is important that the forearms do not cross and that the stick and ball remain in contact with each other throughout the execution of the movement.*

hand turns the stick as if opening a door handle in an anti-clockwise direction. At the same time, the right hand loosens its grip, allowing the shaft to slip around inside it. This way the forearms are able to maintain the same position in relation to each other and, most importantly, they never cross.

In the movement itself, the left hand turns the stick as the right carries its weight beyond the far side of the ball. The stick is then reversed so that its face remains in complete contact with the ball throughout the movement. As the player slows, the flat side of the stick has been twisted in the opposite direction and, as he stops, the back of the stick will be facing forwards. This manoeuvre, executed in an instant, allows the player to change direction and open up new opportunities for his team without ever losing possession.

The key points to remember here are:

- Turn the stick with the left hand only;

- Loosen your right-hand grip to allow the stick to be turned;

- Reverse the stick over and not the ball under.

The Indian Dribble

Stefan Blocker, the West German, is presently one of the finest exponents of the Indian dribble and the sight of him in full flight constantly leaves both spectators and opponents in wonder and amazement. The origins of the technique are rooted in the wizardry of Indian hockey which became the dominant force in the world game from the 1950s and through the 1960s. The ability of the top Indian players to weave around their opponents with ball and stick apparently glued to each other proved a crucial factor in establishing their peerless reputation. Their achievements in that era are made all the more remarkable by the fact that the pitches of the sub-continent were mainly bumpy dust-bowls, although it should be said that these very surfaces must have provided the ultimate challenge and, after mastering them, the grass of Europe, South America and Australasia must have seemed child's play. Similarly, the emergence of the artificial surface, with its true and even contours, has brought about a resurgence of the skill, and the Indian dribble has returned once more to its rightful position as a vital skill for most of the leading players in the modern game.

The movement itself is a refinement of the stop dribble. Here the ball is swept across the body from right to left on the open stick (as in the open dribble), then carried back from left to right by the reverse stick with the player's left hand turned fully in an anti-clockwise direction. If the player is stationary, the ball is carried at right angles to the body, whereas if the move is being executed on the run, the ball is carried across and forward of the player, thus eliminating the risk of his overtaking it. When carried out properly, the ball should be moved over a variety of distances ranging from just a few centimetres from the central line up to a metre or more. The player should practise this particular dribble over a variety of distances and with several changes of speed. This will enable him to adjust exactly how far forward the ball is moved.

Key points to remember here are:

● Move the ball from right to left on the open side;

● Move the ball from left to right on the reverse side;

● Use the left hand to turn the stick, and the right to carry the weight of it;

● Keep the ball moving at right angles to the body when stationary;

● When moving forward, the ball should be moved at an angle in relation to the speed of the player.

Fig. 3 *The Indian dribble: This is a further development of the stop dribble, with the ball carried across the line of the body. The left hand controls the rotational movement of the stick over the ball, while the right hand supports the weight of the stick and carries the stick across the line of the body. Note how the ball is carried across the body from right to left on the open side and then, having fully rotated the left hand anti-clockwise, back across the reverse side. According to the distance the ball is to be carried from side to side, the stick's range of movement should be varied from just a few centimetres either side of a central line to a much greater distance of a metre or more.*

The 'Under the Ball' Dribble

We've already covered the practice of executing the reverse by twisting the stick over the ball, so now we'll take a look at achieving a similar result in a different way. The position of the wrists must be absolutely right for this movement, which relies on the position of the shoulders and a sudden change of pace for maximum effect, although it is a move that is often launched from a standing start. In this particular dribble, the stick is kept behind the ball and is then reversed in a clockwise direction, sliding the face of the stick inside or under the ball. A skilled player can steer the ball in a wide range of directions. Furthermore, a sharp movement to the right (the opponent's left) often leaves the defender completely flat-footed. The 'under the ball' dribble is particularly effective on synthetic surfaces and Sean Kerly is one player who uses it to good effect, as can be seen below.

The under the ball dribble: Sean Kerly of England and Great Britain shows how to put his slightly un-orthodox grip in the under the ball dribble to good effect against West Germany in the World Cup semi-final, 1986. Having carried the ball wide of the diving Schmidt-Opper of Germany, Sean then uses the under the ball dribble to straighten up his run at the approaching Brinkman. To achieve this he has turned his left wrist in a clockwise direction under the ball before re-adjusting his grip to the more orthodox one later in his run. Kerly is a fine example of how adaption and improvisation can create that 'little extra' to achieve success at the highest level.

The Left-handed Dribble

The left-handed dribble: Having carried the ball out wide on his reverse side, Knopp of Scotland moves the ball by a series of nudges around Ireland's McConnel in their 1987 European Cup match. Using a combination of carrying the ball wide of the tackler and then accelerating in behind him, McConnel is effectively cut out. Dribbling the ball on the reverse side requires good arm and wrist strength, in order to carry the stick outstretched in one hand while keeping the ball in reasonably close control away from the defender. It is often used by left-sided players to go wide and around their opponents, with the ball being brought back into a more orthodox dribbling position once they have cut in behind the defender.

The left-handed dribble will never be an easy skill to perfect, but those hours you spend on the practice field trying to come to terms with its demands will stand you in very good stead during the game itself. The left-handed dribble is primarily an option available to those players looking to take the wide route around their opponent's open side. The ball is swept very wide of the body using the reverse side of the stick and then carried either one-handed in a single continuous movement, or alternatively via a series of nudges. It is a movement that requires a great deal of arm and wrist strength and one in which practice really is the only way to make perfect. Executed successfully, the move is a very effective method of running around an opponent. It is a particular favourite with left-sided players, or those making diagonal runs from right to left. The Dutch international Tom Van't Hek is particularly strong on this technique, and it is well worth the novice player taking the trouble to see him in action.

I've deliberately left one vital element of dribbling, and of many other aspects of hockey, until last. The importance of keeping the head up and developing a keen awareness of what is going on around you cannot be overstressed. There are many players at all levels of the game who are capable of demonstrating remarkably high levels of skill when dribbling the ball in practice, yet under match conditions these same players often go completely to pieces and appear mere shadows of their former selves.

After the grip, the other key to successful dribbling is the head. The positioning of the head in relation to the body is vital for balance. However, it is the player's ability to read the game which will more often than not turn out to make that crucial difference between the reasonable club performer and the person who has the capacity to rise higher.

Peripheral vision – or the awareness of everything going on around you – is an ingredient that must never be disregarded. The ball should always be in the bottom line of vision, yet at the same time you should be able to see ahead if you are going to take full advantage of your possession. Fortunately, this is as much an acquired skill as a natural one and practice really can make perfect.

Fig. 4 *Peripheral vision: No matter how adept you are at dribbling the ball, you will not be able to put your possession to effective use unless you can evaluate what is happening to team-mates and opponents around you. As you carry the ball forward you should scan the field, watching out for which passes are available, which defenders are approaching and so on, while still keeping the ball in the bottom line of vision. This wide range of viewing can be improved by practising keeping the eyes up. Since instinct will draw your eyes down to the ball, it is necessary to exaggerate the action of looking over a variety of distances until the head and eyes adopt this 'head up' position naturally.*

THE PUSH

The push is arguably the most important stroke in hockey. Its value lies in its accuracy over both short and intermediate distances, plus the speed with which it can be delivered. Once you have practised the dribble and grown accustomed to your grip and the feeling of moving a hockey ball along the ground in various directions, the push is the next skill you should build into your repertoire.

The push can be used to deliver the ball both as a pass and a shot – the latter is particularly difficult for goalkeepers to deal with because the player with the ball can conceal his intentions until the very last moment. It is essentially a method of passing the ball from one player to another, with speed of action, accuracy and power.

The grip is essentially the same as for the dribble and the ball should be positioned in line with the right shoulder. To execute the manoeuvre, you should move the left hand forward in the direction the ball is to be pushed. Then, by maintaining your grip and stance, the right hand should be swept through much more quickly with the effect of catapulting the ball forward. The crucial element in achieving both power and precision from this movement is keeping the head down over the ball and ensuring that the stick pushes right through the intended line. The stick should end up pointing in the direction that the ball has been pushed. Good pushers – like Jon Potter, the England and Great Britain international for example – adopt a low body position with the knees bent and maintain this stance throughout the execution. His smoothness of execution, and excellent timing combined with a good follow-through, are a trademark of Jon's game.

The power of the push will be determined by the speed of the stick head as it passes through the ball. This power is generated by the right leg and is then transferred into the stick through the right shoulder and arm.

Fig. 5 *The push: The 'power supply' for this manoeuvre is supplied by the legs driving through the ball. The body, forearms and wrists utilise this force, pushing through the line of the ball with constant accelera-tion. The actual movement of the stick is led by the top hand, with the lower hand accelerating past, creating a levering effect. A low body position, with the head over the ball, and a smooth action with a strong follow-through, are the keys to success in this skill.*

Pushing to the Left and Right

By opening and closing the blade of the stick, small variations can be made to the direction in which the ball travels. Closing the blade has the effect of dragging the ball to the left of the normal line of travel; opening it pushes the ball outside. Merely opening or closing the blade of the stick, however, achieves only a limited change of direction. Without some co-operation from the body, the ball will soon slip or slice away from the target line. What is needed is a rotational movement from the waist to align the shoulders with the direction in which you wish the ball to travel. In simple terms, if you wish the ball to go further, either to the right or to the left, you should bring the left shoulder to point in the new direction of the ball. Whatever that direction is, the stick must continue to accelerate in the same way as the original push, straight through the line of the ball's trajectory.

The push – following through: James Duthie of England and Great Britain shows how to push the ball with accuracy and control. Having kept his head over the ball and maintained a low body position through-out the stroke, the power generated by this back leg has been transferred through the stick to the ball. On completion of the movement the stick has travelled through the line of the push, to end up pointing in the direction of the ball.

Feinting and Pushing Right or Left

Once you have mastered the basic push you will quickly realise that the position of the shoulders offers the clearest indication of a player's intentions. The next step, therefore, is to find a way of successfully disguising the direction of the stroke. The most effective way to achieve this is by way of the feint. Here the player changes the direction of the stick's head by exaggerating the movement of the right arm in relation to the position of the shoulder, that is pointing the shoulder in one direction but pushing the forearm and stick through a completely different line. Strength and timing are the two key factors if the movement is to be completed successfully; however, the basic principle of the stick head travelling right through the intended line of delivery does still apply.

You must acknowledge that the movement described is an advanced technique. A considerable amount of power is lost without the full use of the strength from the right leg and shoulder; nevertheless, when carried out successfully this move can prove very useful as a way of deceiving an opponent about your true intentions.

Pushing off the Wrong Foot

Most pushing movements are executed from a stationary or slow-moving position. To attempt the push on the run would, for the most part, almost certainly lead to the player falling over at the end of the movement. However, a player can use the momentum of running when he is pushing off the 'wrong' (i.e. the right) foot. This is no technique for beginners – it takes a lot of practice to develop, and the key factor is balance.

In this movement the ball is pushed with the player running at speed. The ball should be level with the right foot and one of the important factors to remember is that, in common with all the push strokes, the face of the stick should be in contact with the ball for as long as possible. It is almost a case of the stick chasing the ball until the parting comes with the stick pointing in the direction of trajectory. The momentum of movement should enable you to deliver the pushed pass or shot to your chosen angle by pivoting on the right foot. In the case of the shot, this makes the intended direction even more difficult to read because the player in possession can mask his plans until the final moment. Passing, too, can be timed with much more effect.

I've already warned that this is a difficult skill to perfect, but that certainly doesn't mean you shouldn't try. Once you have the confidence to use it under match conditions, you will find it a most useful addition to your repertoire.

(OVERLEAF) Pushing off the right foot: In this Junior International between England and France, the English attacker has led the defender to believe that he was passing across his open side. With the ball outside the line of his right leg, he has rotated his waist and shoulders to 'open out' the reverse side of the defender. Using the momentum of the ball, he accelerates his right arm through the ball and along the new direction of travel. A fine example of combining a little deception with refined skills.

The key points about the push are as follows:

● Keep your head over the ball but your eyes up at all times;

● Push the right leg up through the right shoulder and down through the right arm;

● Push right through the ball with the stick, ensuring that you complete the movement with it pointing in the direction the ball has gone.

STOPPING THE BALL

An ability to stop the ball quickly would seem fundamental to successful hockey yet, surprisingly, it often proves to be the weak point of many otherwise accomplished players. Failure to stop or trap the ball properly leaves the player floundering, unable to capitalise on any of the other possession skills he may have perfected. What is more, it is those vital moments lost while struggling to bring the ball under control which make the difference between the player who appears to have all the time in the world when in possession and the one who seems flustered and rushed in everything he does.

The master of this sort of control is undoubtedly the Australian, Treva King. If you see him in action, watch the way he receives the ball and then sweeps it into position for his next move all in the same fluid movement. By demonstrating his confidence and absolute ability at all times, he appears to create extra time for himself and therefore his team-mates too.

As with the dribble or the push, the brain has a vital role to play in successful trapping. Often the player's next intended move will determine the way in which he approaches the task of getting the ball under control, so it is important to keep thinking ahead at all times. Head and body position too, along with balance, are important factors while steadiness of head and eye cannot be over-emphasised.

Stopping the Ball from the Front with a Vertical Stick

The orthodox grip – something you should be getting increasingly familiar with by now – remains the correct position for this manoeuvre, but be sure to keep your hands well apart. The knees and the body should also be slightly bent. The stick should be moved along the same line as the approaching ball, and control is achieved by pulling back on the lower hand leaving the upper one slightly forward, presenting the stick with a downward slant. The effect of this will be twofold. On the one hand it will serve to deflect the ball downwards, while at the same time the 'give' in the right hand will help absorb the impact and in doing so take the power out of the ball.

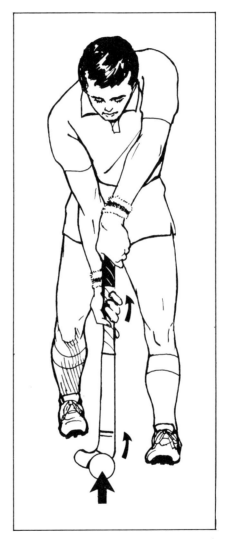

Fig. 6 *Stopping the ball from the front: The technique of stopping the ball cleanly from straight ahead is dependent on a good body position. With the feet apart and staggered slightly, it is possible to achieve a head-above-hands-above-ball position. The stick is withdrawn along the line of the approaching ball, with the left hand remaining firm while the lower (right) hand 'gives' on impact to absorb the momentum of the ball. By keeping body weight well forward, the player can transfer the ball into a new position in a simultaneous movement, rather than with the series of jerky actions often associated with receiving the ball.*

When stopping the ball from the front, the head, hands, stick and feet should all be in line with the path of the ball. If, in practice, you find that the ball tends to edge off the stick, you should check that your head position is correct. Get that wrong and you'll find it difficult to bring the ball under control cleanly, even on the most flawless surface; get it right, and the movement will seem simple and soon become almost second nature.

Stopping the Ball to the Sides

Under match play conditions, it is often better to receive the ball to the sides of the body. This way a player can put himself in a more advantageous position for executing the next move. Collecting to the side also enables the player to take the ball in his stride and gain valuable yards on his opponent. Essentially, the key to this skill is the positioning of eye, hands and stick head – keep all three in line and you will find that there is very little difference in receiving the ball, whether it be to the open or reverse sides.

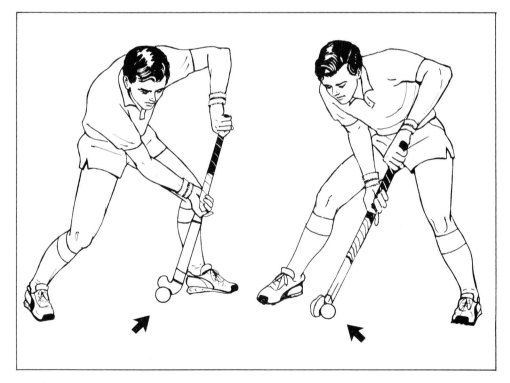

Fig. 7 *Stopping the ball to the left and right on the open stick: Stopping the ball from the sides follows the same principle as from the front: the knees should be bent and the head – and therefore body weight – kept forward. Try to keep the foot on the side to which the ball is travelling, in front of the line of the body, as this will help to keep the head in line with the ball, thus reducing the number of angles to be calculated and simplifying the whole operation.*

The reverse side, however, does mean a minimal reduction in the surface area of the stick. That said, the stick should be turned as in the reverse side dribble to enable the ball to be collected underneath the line of the head and the hands. If the ball is miscued, it is often as a direct result of the player failing to observe this basic rule.

Fig. 8 *Stopping the ball to the reverse side: Although in principle no more difficult than any other stopping skill, there is more room for error on the reverse side because of the reduction in stopping area and the judgement of different angles and speeds involved. The stick is reversed by fully rotating the left wrist; the stick is then carried along the line of the approaching ball by the right hand. Again, by trying to achieve a head-over-ball position with the body weight well forward, the number of angles to be judged are reduced and in addition the bottom hand acts as a kind of shock absorber.*

Having looked at receiving the ball on both sides, it is fair to say that the majority of players do prefer to collect the ball from the left and onto the open side. The main reason for this is that the head of the stick and the eyes tend to fall naturally in line with the ball's trajectory.

Whether stationary or moving, successful trapping stems from balancing and timing. Furthermore, by moving the stick down the line of the approaching ball it becomes easier to judge its approach and angle.

Practise the skill from a stationary position until you feel confident you have got the timing right, then move onto the next stage by attempting the same manoeuvre on the run. This is when really first class control can count in a match.

Laying Down the Stick

This is a skill which has become more and more useful to hockey players since the advent of artificial surfaces, be they the synthetic outdoor type or the wooden floors utilised in the indoor game. The artificial surface enables the ball to run true and therefore allows the player to command a greater area of the pitch when attempting to collect the loose ball. Laying down the stick has developed into such a useful technique that it has even influenced the development of the stick itself.

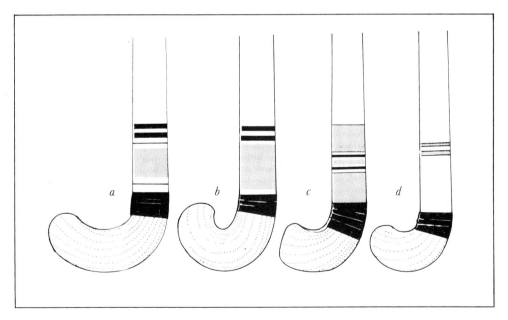

Fig. 9 *Development of the hockey stick: The changing game of hockey and the ever-increasing use of artificial turf has led to a plethora of ideas and innovations in hockey stick design. Fig. a shows the typical shape of the stick at the end of the 'grass hockey era' (c. 1978); figs b, c and d illustrate some of today's most popular designs, which allow greater power to be imparted through the stick head and which facilitate the artificial turf-type skills such as laying the stick down. Note the reduction in the length of head.*

Essentially this is a one-handed skill with the stick often released with the right hand. Stopping the ball to the open side, the player slides the stick along the ground with the intention of using the long barrier created to stop the ball. The left hand should be as close to the ground as possible (a matter of centimetres preferably), so this involves the player bending very low. The distance you need to reach will determine which foot is nearer the ball.

Fig. 10 *Stopping the ball very wide on the open side: A very low body position enables the player to cover some two or three metres to either side. With one leg forward and the head in a low position, the stick is slid along the turf to intercept across the line of the ball. By lowering the left hand to a height just off the ground, a large area can be covered by the full length of the stick. Tilting the toe of the stick slightly forward helps to prevent the ball from bouncing up into the air.*

In international matches it is not uncommon to see players diving to reach a ball way to the side of them. However, it is not a move to be recommended at club level because mis-timing could leave a side particularly vulnerable to attack.

Laying down the stick on the reverse side can be more difficult because the success of the manoeuvre is determined by the way in which the stick is turned by the wrist. Again the fingers should be very close to – if not actually touching – the ground.

Laying down the stick has been a contributory factor in the trend towards reducing the size of the stick head. Had this modification not been made, the ball could have easily slipped between the toe and the bridge, leaving the player stretched and stranded with the ball running past him. Although the advanced design makes this unlikely, the possibility can be avoided and the trapping technique improved by turning the left wrist slightly in a clockwise direction to use the face of the stick to pin the ball in a wedge. The key to success is in getting the body down low and the fingers almost on the ground.

Fig. 11 *The reverse stick 'trap' – laying the stick down: When the ball is travelling smoothly along the ground the player can stop the ball over a much greater distance by adopting a very low body position, with the fingers of the left hand near or on the ground. Again the head and body weight should be well forward, with the stick held firmly and tilted towards the oncoming ball. This wide area reduces the necessity for calculating the exact path of the ball which, once trapped, can be dragged back in front of the body by tilting the stick even further and sweeping the stick from left to right.*

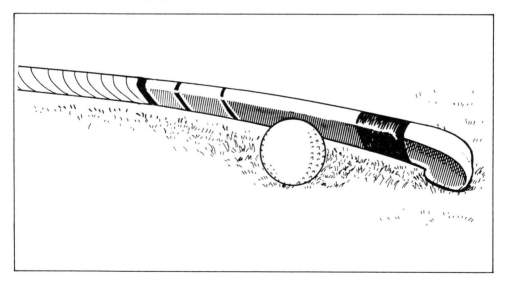

Fig. 12 *The reverse stick wedge for stopping the ball: By laying the stick down and tilting the stick forwards, a wedge can be achieved which will trap the ball travelling across a flat surface. The large area covered by this technique makes this skill an easy and very effective way of controlling the ball wide on the reverse side. The shortening of the stick head in recent years has enabled players to achieve a much higher success rate in this skill.*

Receiving the Ball in the Air

Strange though it may seem to the uninitiated, if the hockey ball flies at a player the laws of the game will not allow him to attempt a baseball-type hit at it. Instead he must try to play the ball down onto the ground.

If you're directly in line with the ball, the principles are the same as for trapping the ball from the front. The grip, head and body position are all the same, but because of the flight of the ball the right hand is in front of the left offering the face of the stick at right angles to the flight of the ball. As the ball strikes, the right hand gives a little, thus absorbing the momentum and dropping the ball in front of the player. If the eyes are in line with the ball, this is the safest way of executing the manoeuvre. Alternatively, once the ball has been cushioned and is still in contact with the stick, a player can push through it to change direction and fend off any close challenge.

Stopping the ball in the air from the front: Richard Dodds, the England and Great Britain captain, demonstrates the ideal technique for receiving the ball in the air. Keeping his head and weight well forward, with feet slightly staggered, he keeps his eyes, hands and stick behind the line of the ball. The slightly modified grip of the right hand allows him either to 'take the ball in,' playing it down to the ground by his feet, or to push out with his arms on impact and re-direct the ball away from an oncoming opponent.

Clearly it is not always possible to put the body behind the line of the ball. Under these circumstances the stick should be held horizontally on the open or reverse side. The cardinal rule is to keep your eyes on the ball at all times.

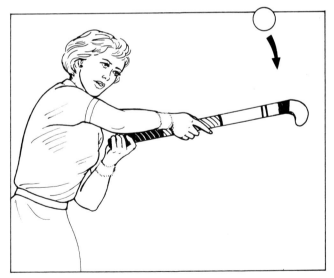

Fig. 13 *Stopping the ball in the air to the open and reverse side: In situations where it is not possible to position yourself directly behind the line of the ball, you must try and judge the flight of the ball so that you can receive it between waist and chest height. The stick should be in a horizontal position, head and body weight steady. The technique then follows that of the other stopping skills, with the lower hand absorbing the power from the ball.*

Some players practise juggling exercises with the stick and ball. This helps them to develop a better judgement for angles and speed and, naturally, it also helps build confidence for match conditions.

Receiving the Ball when Closely Marked by an Opponent

If you are about to receive the ball with an opponent in close attention, it is probably not wise to attempt to stop it because you may well be offering him the opportunity to steal the ball away from you. Under these circumstances one of the most effective ploys is to absorb most of the ball's speed and then redirect the remaining momentum by carrying the stick – with the ball in contact – beyond the opponent. This movement is recognised as close control and represents a fluid demonstration of most of the skills covered in this chapter. In fig. 14 the ball has been partially stopped, the player has used her vision to determine her next move and, with the ball in close contact, has succeeded in turning away from the point of danger.

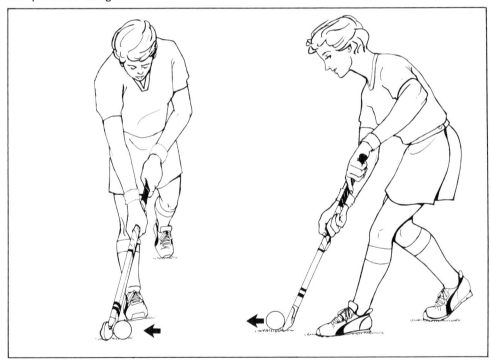

Fig. 14 *Receiving the ball when closely marked: No great magic powers are needed to create that little extra space and time when receiving the ball. By integrating in one smooth, controlled motion, the two skills of stopping the ball and dribbling the ball forward, using a sway of the hips and the drive of the back foot you can move yourself and the ball beyond your opponent in the same time it normally takes to stop the ball dead. Practise with the ball coming to you at a variety of angles and speeds, until the ball is absorbed and flows with your balanced movement.*

Stopping the ball: Although the Dutch attack are in a very threatening position in their World Cup ('86) match, the Spanish defender has used the low stopping technique to cover a large surface area to intercept the attacker's pass. Notice the good balanced 'stopping' position of the other players, with their heads and body weight well forward.

The points to remember about stopping the ball are as follows:

• Pay particular attention to the positioning of head, eyes and body;

• Make sure your grip is right to enable you to execute the manoeuvres;

• Practise regularly to build confidence and learn to judge the speed and flight of the ball.

THE HIT

Primarily the hit is used as a way of passing the ball over greater distances, moving from defence to attack, switching play from one flank to the other. It is also applied over shorter distances when a player finds himself in space and therefore with enough time to pick his spot, and, of course, it can be used to devastating effect around goal.

Hockey is no different from any other bat and ball game when it comes to hitting the ball – the good striker combines power and stick speed with impeccable timing. Thinking about this skill, I'm drawn to players like Carsten Fischer of West Germany. You have to understand that at the highest level, players like Fischer are hitting a ball 7.5 cm in diameter with the head of a stick which is only around 5 cm wide. Yet, with a combination of power and technique, they can achieve speeds well in excess of 100 mph.

In the light of all this it may seem surprising that this combination of complex skills may result only in disappointment when applied to the shot at goal. The stroke's main disadvantage is in the time it takes to set up. This may be only a fraction of a second in real terms, but enough to enable the goalkeeper to interpret the direction of the shot and take steps to cover it. To overcome this handicap, the forward must show some guile, often with intricate footwork to disguise his intentions.

Hitting a Stationary Ball

With the exception of the slap hit, which we'll deal with later in the chapter, hitting is one of the skills where the grip on the stick is modified to ensure maximum effect. In the hit sequence the hands come together, with the right sliding up to join the left close to the top of the stick. There are players who use a slightly more wristy action, sliding both hands into position some 10 or 15 cms from the top, but this is mainly to enable them to reduce the amount of back-swing required and therefore speed up the execution of the manoeuvre. In my view, the leverage involved justifies keeping the hands at the top of the stick because it maximises head speed through the ball. With the ball either in line with, or just behind, the front foot, the player should ensure his weight is positioned over it. If the ball is too far away from the body, the stick head will create a spinning effect on the ball when it makes contact.

With the perfect hit, the stick is swept backwards behind the body and then brought forward as quickly as possible with the weight of the right hand pushing through the accelerating stick head. It is important to keep a tight grip on the stick to prevent twisting when it makes contact with the ball. However, at a more

The hit: Ekhard Schmidt-Opper of West Germany demonstrates how a combination of timing and technique can impart great power. With the ball to the side and ahead of the front foot, he has accelerated the stick head by transferring the power exerted through his legs to his body and into his arms. His forearm strength is much in evidence, as is his concentration on the ball at the moment of impact.

advanced level, twisting can be deliberately introduced to the hit to change the direction of the ball and disguise the striker's intentions. By twisting the grip in a clockwise direction (opening the face) the ball can be sliced off to the right. Twisting in an anti-clockwise direction has the effect of pulling the ball to the left.

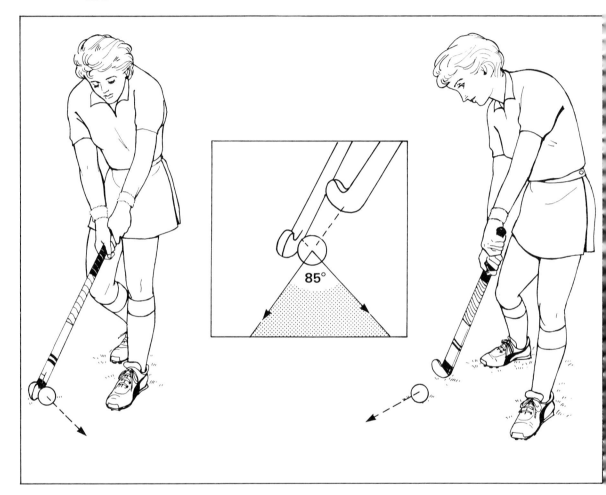

Fig. 15 *Changing the angle of the hit: A combination of twisting the wrists and changing the arc of the hit enables the ball to be hit over a much greater range of angles. By turning the wrists in an anti-clockwise direction, closing the face of the stick and widening the arc of the stick away from the body, the ball can be hit inside (i.e. from right to left). By opening the wrists, opening the face of the stick and bringing the arc of the stick inside the ball, the ball can be 'sliced' out from left to right. Flexibility of the wrists, combined with good timing, produces a clean, accurate hit.*

Some players adopt a grip lower down the stick to achieve this skill with greater accuracy. These type of passes or shots can be very effective at deceiving an opponent about one's intentions, but require one's full concentration if they are to be executed effectively.

The speed of the hit is achieved through a combination of transferring the body weight from the back to the front foot and the acceleration of the stick head. Keeping the eyes on the ball is vital for successful execution and you must resist the temptation to look in the direction the ball is going before the stick has actually made contact with the target. The result is invariably a mis-hit.

Hitting on the Run

The techniques of grip and body position are the same for hitting the ball on the run as they are for striking from a static position. To ensure success, however, it is important to ensure that the ball is positioned slightly in front of the left foot. From here you can influence both the direction of the ball and its trajectory. To hit from right to left the stick should be swung away from the body, i.e. around the ball. To lift or undercut, the ball should be allowed to run further in front of the foot and during the downswing the wrists should be turned fully in a clockwise direction to completely open the face of the stick.

In effect, the stroke cuts underneath the ball, swinging through and across on a right to left arc. The more open the face and the further under the ball, the higher the trajectory. The chip hit is a refinement of this technique and I will describe it later.

Hitting off the Wrong Foot

Sometimes when the ball has to be hit from left to right, the player cannot afford the luxury in terms of time of getting his or her feet all the way around and in front of the ball. The alternative is to leave the ball behind and then play it close to the back foot.

For this movement, the shoulders are turned in a clockwise direction to face the direction of the hit. The stick is then swung in an arc with the opening or closing of the face of the stick determining the exact line the ball will take. Clearly, with a manoeuvre as difficult as this one, it is important for the eyes to remain firmly fixed on the ball.

The Slap Hit

This skill can best be described as a combination of the techniques of pushing and hitting, and it has been developed to perfection by some of the finest players in the world.

The stick is held as if for the push with the hands well apart, then on the downward swing the weight is transferred from the back to the front foot. At the moment of contact the top (left) hand is brought back towards the body while the bottom (right) accelerates even more quickly through the ball. The levering effect can produce remarkable power from a relatively short backswing and, because the action is particularly quick, requiring no change in the hand or body position, it is swift in its execution and relatively easy to disguise.

Fig. 16 *Hitting off the wrong foot: There are many occasions when a player wishes to hit the ball from left to right on the run, but has neither the time nor the room to get their feet around and past the ball. The same technique as that shown in fig. 15 is used, slicing the ball from left to right with the arc of the stick coming inside the ball – but this time the ball is hit on the run just outside of the right leg. This enables the shot to be played in a balanced position while on the move.*

The slap hit: Hasan Sadar, Pakistan's Olympic Gold medal centre-forward, demonstrates the use of the slap hit against the author in their World Cup pool match (London 1986). Although he has the very close attention of England full-back David Faulkner, by changing his hand positions he still manages to achieve great power and accuracy with this combined hitting/pushing stroke, without losing valuable time.

The Chip Hit

With the advent of the artificial playing surface the chip hit is a more widely used technique. The spongy nature of the surface has allowed players to develop techniques enabling them to hit passes covering one-half to two-thirds of the field and over the top of their opponents. In essence, the chip hit is an exaggerated version of that applied when undercutting the ball. Here the ball is allowed to run a little further in front of the player, who leans back with his weight over the back foot. The face of the stick is opened up and the ball is struck from as far underneath as possible. If you can imagine almost hitting the ground beneath the ball then you will have some idea of the angle. The stick itself is swung in an arc from the outside (right) to the inside (left) and this introduces a considerable amount of backspin which in turn creates greater elevation and distance. Again, the eyes are important because you must avoid either getting a thin edge or toeing the ball, which will only result in sending it at great speed at head height and probably in the direction of an opponent – not a pretty sight on a public park on a winter's afternoon when the ambulance can't plough through the mud to reach the injured player! The inherent dangers of this particular skill are obvious and therefore I would implore you to employ it in real match circumstances only after hours of careful practice.

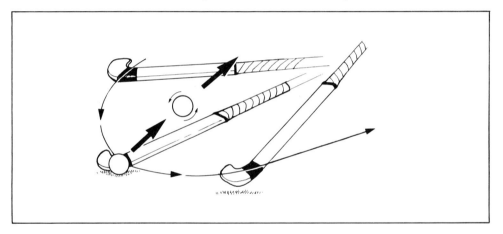

Fig. 17 *The chip hit: By bringing the stick in a very low arc with the wrists well open, and hitting underneath the ball, the chip hit can produce both elevation – due to its backspin – and distance. This is most certainly a stroke where practice makes perfect.*

I have paid a lot of attention to the artificial surface and the role it has enjoyed in transforming our game. Therefore, within the context of this particular chapter, it would seem only fair to describe a special form of hit that could not ordinarily have been performed on grass. I'm talking about the 'squeeze' and I suppose it would be wrong to even give it a sub-heading of its own because this skill is a hybrid developed by some of the world's finest players and based on their individual experience of these conditions.

Often the artificial surface has a spongy, grass-like quality on top with a firm base beneath. Those who have learned how to perfect the technique find they can literally 'squeeze' the ball into the air. This is a tactic frequently used by forwards hoping to take advantage of an advancing goalkeeper. The secret is to leave the ball behind almost in line with the back foot. To execute the manoeuvre the player hits down on the upper half of the ball with the face of the stick closed. This has the effect of squeezing the ball through the soft upper surface and launching it up off the hard surface below. Those who've perfected this move time it to perfection by locking the left forearm to avoid vibration on the stick and therefore increase its momentum. Once mastered, the ball should travel in a dipping arc.

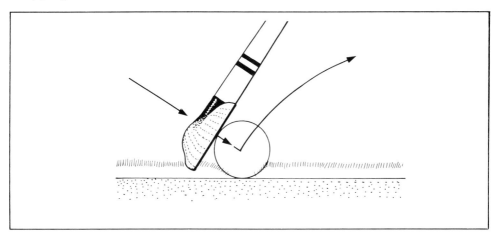

Fig. 18 *Squeezing the ball: Using the inherent qualities of the artificial surface, a 'hitting down' action on the ball has the effect of sending it through the air in a dipping arc. Forearm and wrist strength are crucial factors in this stroke.*

The points to learn from this chapter are as follows:

● Timing is vitally important, so be sure to practise as much as possible;

● Adapt the correct form of hit for each situation, depending on circumstances;

● Consider the element of danger before hitting the ball into the air;

● Practise hitting the ball when in an ideal position and in more inconvenient ones;

● Try to create a feeling of smoothness when hitting the ball, rather than a rushed, snatching movement;

● Technique needs a considerable amount of work because power alone is never going to beat an experienced goalkeeper.

THE FLICK

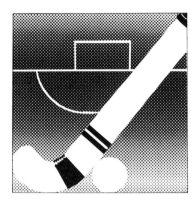

The flick is a versatile stroke, best summed up as a specialised form of push which lifts the ball up into the air whether it be a few centimetres over an opponent's stick, high into the net, or over some distance, clearing an opponent's head. It is a skill which is playing an ever-increasing role in hockey as the game develops and becomes more tactical.

The aerial flick is a means of getting the ball beyond a packed opposition. Executed properly, it can allow a free-running forward the opportunity to go straight for goal. Ties Kruze, the Dutchman, would regularly 'throw' 50- or 60-metre aerial passes, allowing his side to switch from defence under pressure to attack with opportunity at a flick of his wrists. In all standards of the game, the aerial flick is an increasingly popular stroke – primarily because it is such an effective pass.

Flicking a Stationary Ball

Spectators often see the flick as 'a throwing of the ball' and, to be fair, from the sidelines that must be how the manoeuvre appears. From the player's point of view, the objective is to get the stick under the ball and keep it in contact for as long as possible. The hands are held apart in a similar fashion to the push and the movement is always executed with the ball well ahead of the front (left) foot.

The player bends very low on the back (right) foot and positions the stick underneath the ball. As he moves forward to carry it onto the face of the stick the top hand is pulled back towards the body as the lower hand is swept rapidly forward. This momentum is greatly increased by driving off the back foot (see picture of Jon Potter opposite) – a manoeuvre which requires precise timing if it is to be executed successfully.

Flicking the ball: Jon Potter of England and Great Britain (left) demonstrates the effortless technique that makes him one of the best flickers of the ball in the game today. Highlighted in this shot is the way he uses the transfer of body weight from right to left foot to generate power for the stroke.

In the next stage of the flick, demonstrated by Delissen of Holland (right), the ball is carried on the stick for as long as possible. With the drive off the back leg generating power through a low body position, it is possible to 'throw' aerials of some 40 – 60 metres. By keeping the head forward and down – as Delissen does here – a smooth co-ordinated action will lead to successful flicking.

Flicking on the Run

The technique for the flick on the run is broadly similar to the movement described above. However, it is important to stress that the body should maintain its momentum through the entire stroke. The left hand should be almost in contact with the right forearm, transforming the stick into a long lever – almost an extension of the right arm itself.

The momentum of body and stick must be kept going throughout, in order to ensure that the ball doesn't roll off the toe of the stick as it is lifted by the action of the arm and shoulder.

Reverse Stick Flicking

It is often difficult to differentiate between the reverse stick flick and the reverse stick push. With the ball on the reverse side, the right foot is usually forward, giving better body balance. However, this is one move where the same effect can probably be achieved with either foot. The head is positioned over the ball and the left hand is pushed away from the line the ball is to take. Simultaneously the right hand pulls rapidly through the ball carrying it off on the stick head.

There is a problem of comfort with this manoeuvre and most players find it easier to execute at the end of an 'under the ball' dribble. This enables the player to use the lever of his right arm more effectively and therefore keep the stick in contact with the ball for longer periods.

This is undoubtedly a complex skill and many players never master it, but for those with the patience to try, the end result will be all the more rewarding. Essentially, a large proportion of contact with the ball should be on the reverse side, yet for many this is an area of great weakness. Timing and good position are all important, and practice will bring its rewards.

The Scoop

Scooping or shovelling is often the easiest way for the beginner to get the ball into the air. It is an action largely defunct in the modern game since the advent of synthetic pitches, yet, at the same time, one that should be retained within the armoury of every player because the scoop can produce a ball with a high trajectory while covering a relatively short distance. Goalkeepers are particularly vulnerable to the scoop on the run at the top of the circle. The usual grip for the push or dribble is employed and the actual move is brought off with the right foot forward and to the outside of the ball. As the player bends low, the right hand comes forward and the effect on the stick is to dig forward under the ball, with the right shoulder turning in the direction the ball is to travel.

Flicking the ball is essentially a right-handed skill and therefore it can be a useful practice to take the left hand off the stick and try to 'lift and throw' with just the right hand. It soon becomes obvious that with the stick acting as an extension of the right arm, the feeling of throwing or slinging the ball is the key to successful flicking.

Fig. 19 (LEFT) *The reverse stick flick: With the margins for error so fine, a good head position is undoubtedly the key to success in reverse stick flicking. The mechanics are the same as for an ordinary flick, with the operation carried out across the line of the body from left to right and the ball carried on the reverse stick for as long as possible. This is a skill that obviously needs much practice and total concentration if it is to be completed successfully.*

Fig. 20 *The scoop: Scooping the ball is used less frequently as the game moves away from boggy grass pitches to today's artificial turf. The reasons for its demise are the long time it can take to carry out the manoeuvre and the obviousness of the player's intentions. It is, however, a very effective and simple way of getting the ball in the air, particularly for youngsters. By 'digging' under the ball (as with a shovel) and rapidly bringing the lower hand upwards, the ball is carried for as long as possible on the stick. Due to the arc the stick travels through, the ball rises in a very steep trajectory, making this shot effective against an onrushing goalkeeper.*

Points to remember from this chapter are as follows:

• The power is generated initially from the legs, through the trunk and to the forearms and wrists;

• Try to maintain a low body position, with the head well forward;

• Aim to achieve a smooth, flowing action, with a positive follow-through;

• Get the feeling of 'carrying' the ball on the stick.

BEATING AN OPPONENT

The player in possession has two options when trying to go past an opponent. The first is the wall pass with a team-mate, the player originating the move running beyond the defender to receive the return ball, and the second, and perhaps more risky, is the dribble.

While the surest and easiest method of beating an opponent will be to pass the ball around him, there are inevitably movements within the game when an individual's guile and technical skill will be put to the test in a one-versus-one situation. When two players of comparable skill face up to each other the contest becomes a battle of wits, with the tackler trying to set up his opponent in such a way that he is able to steal the ball. At the same time, the attacker is trying to throw the defender with a combination of body feints and ball movements, each designed to tempt the tackler into committing himself recklessly and in so doing make the all-important mistake and allow the man with the ball to get through.

Among youngsters, where the physical differences between two players may be much greater, it can be possible for one player to beat another simply by speed alone. Indeed, even at international level this particular asset has often been demonstrated to considerable effect. Perhaps one of its finest exponents was Samiulla Khan of Pakistan – one of the game's all-time greats. In the 1970s he dominated this aspect of the game and thrilled crowds the world over simply by 'throwing' the ball past his opponent and then with a devastating turn of pace accelerating into the space behind him and on towards goal.

Of my own contemporaries, one player above others exemplifies all the characteristics of balance and control coupled with an ability to go around his opponent in either direction. Ric Charlesworth of Australia has been described by many as the 'perfect player' and anyone who has seen him on top form will be hard pushed to dispute the accolade.

Beating an opponent: Ric Charlesworth of Australia cuts into the heart of the Pakistani defence in Perth, Australia. With stick and ball seemingly glued to each other, he weaves through the opposition, committing defenders into rash tackles.

Deceiving an Opponent

The player in possession should ideally be travelling at half to two-thirds of his normal sprinting speed. This leaves him with all his options intact when it comes to the defender's challenge. He should have his head down over the ball but – mindful of the value of peripheral vision – should have his eyes looking upwards. The ball should be as close to the stick as possible to eliminate the possibility of an unexpected 'steal'.

The main objective as the defender closes in is to dupe him into believing you are going to do one thing when your real intention is to do something completely different. This can be achieved by a 'dummy' push of the ball or a combination of body feints and swerves. All have the same objective – to move the defender in one direction while you move the opposite way and into an empty space. Sounds simple, doesn't it! It's a bit harder when you're actually out there on the pitch but, as with all of the skills I have described within these pages, practice makes perfect. Most players work on a combination of skills, blending body movements with ball actions to create a series of alternative ways of squeezing past their opponent. Many players have a natural inclination to favour one side or the other, but at the highest level of the game this can only lead to a certain predictability and therefore weakness in style, and should be resisted whenever possible.

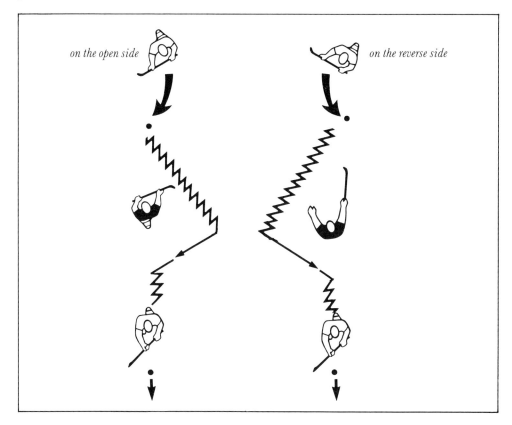

Fig. 21 *Going round an opponent: Approaching the defender at about two-thirds of his maximum speed, the attacker appears to be going around him one side, before sharply cutting back and accelerating past the defender on the other. Once past, the player with the ball moves in behind the defender to close him out of the game, restricting any further intervention. A combination of guile and speed off the mark produce a formula for successfully taking opponents on.*

Going Around an Opponent

When dribbling down the right or reverse side, the first objective is to convince the tackler that you are going to make your move on the opponent's open side. Assuming this has been achieved, the change of direction must be executed with precise timing to throw the other player onto the wrong foot. Speed off the mark is essential and so is the need to maintain control of the ball. This can be achieved either with the stick and ball in close contact, or by throwing the ball out wide of the defender's reach.

Dribbling to the left or on the 'open side' is even more reliant on the attacking player's strength of conviction and ability to throw the defender off balance at the crucial point of the manoeuvre. Here it may be necessary to move the defender several metres to the left before wrong-footing him with a sudden pull inside.

Whatever the way past, it is important that as soon as the attacking player clears the defender he should slip back into line directly behind him. This not only helps with speed, but also prevents the quick turn and recovery which could otherwise enable the defender to get in a second challenge. Those players who look as if they are making a move around their opponent only to find they have merely been forced into another area of the field are on the way to handing control of the situation to their opponent.

The combination of a balanced, controlled approach – a feint or a dummy and then acceleration to the side and behind the opponent – is one of the most complex combinations of skills in the game. International players spend years

Going round an opponent's open stick: Diepveen of Holland shows both pace and control as he commits the defender into a rash tackle attempt. Having carried the ball out wide of the defender's tackle attempt, he accelerates away with stick and ball in tandem.

practising and go on practising every time they take to the training field. The next time you watch an international and see these manoeuvres demonstrated, don't say 'How do they do it?' but ask yourself: 'I wonder if I can do that?'

Points to remember from this chapter are as follows:

• Beating an opponent is a combination of ball skills and deception;

• Keep the stick and ball in strong contact as you pass your opponent;

• Commit the defender to an action or movement, and then use your stick skills to carry the ball away from the tackle;

• As soon as the opponent is beaten, cut in behind him or her to prevent further intervention.

Cutting in behind the defender: Hasan Sadar, the Pakistan Olympic centre-forward, has dazzled spectators and defenders the world over with the speed with which he transfers the ball from one side to the other to go round an opponent. Having carried the ball wide of the Canadian's lunging tackle, Sadar cuts quickly back in to rule out any further intervention by the defender.

TACKLING

One of the most satisfying elements of hockey for the outfield player is the feeling of having pulled off that vital tackle – whether it be a carefully-controlled, good, firm interception to the front of the body or an unorthodox, last-second lunge that nicks the ball away to safety just as the striker is moving into the circle and shaping to shoot.

There are three basic areas in which the tackle is made: to the front of the body with the opponent bearing down on you head-on; to the open-side or in other words your stick hand; and on the reverse side, i.e. to the left of your body.

Regardless of where the tackle is to be made, there remain a number of basic rules to help in the successful execution of the movement. The first is a strong body position, and by this I mean balance. Timing the tackle is also vital because in most instances your opponent will have the ball under control and therefore some idea of the way he intends to manoeuvre around you. You should not commit yourself unless you believe you have a more than fifty-fifty chance of success, and until that point is reached you should be prepared to back off and allow the player with the ball to advance. At the same time you should be looking to restrict the area into which he can move. Many coaches preach that you should 'tackle with your legs' by running with the opponent. You must always be prepared to change direction quickly should the forward attempt to throw you off balance with a feint or swerve, so you must never allow yourself to become either flat-footed or square on to the player with the ball.

When you make the tackle, do so strongly and with confidence because second thoughts at this stage will leave you beaten and stranded. If you come away with the ball it is important to gain control of it quickly and play it away to a team-mate in space. The well-timed tackle, leaving the defender in control, often provides the springboard for a rapid counter-attack.

Tackling in Front of the Body with a Flat Stick

This is perhaps the most basic of the conventional tackles and is used to counter the opponent running directly at the defender. Strength and timing are the crucial factors. Close down the space available to the player with the ball, then at the moment you choose to make the tackle, throw your body weight forward and thrust the stick firmly through the ball, making sure that its angle covers as much ground as possible to ensure the maximum chance of success. With the ball safely in your possession, get it under control quickly and look for that next pass.

Tackling on the Open Side

This is the tackle to make if your opponent has already committed himself to running around your right-hand side, and again timing will play a vital part in your chances of success. The player with the ball will usually be in total control and pushing forward hard in an effort to shake off your challenge. The important thing is to get alongside him – if you try to make your tackle too soon you run the risk of colliding with his body or stick and causing an infringement.

At the point of the tackle you should drop your body into a low position and get the stick close to the ground to present as large a solid obstacle as possible, thus using the power of your legs and forearms to the full. You should time your tackle for the point when the ball is furthest away from your opponent's stick and therefore technically out of his control. Bring it away with a dragging movement, then get your right hand back onto the stick as quickly as possible and move away.

Many coaches instruct their players to 'tackle with their legs', that is to run with the opponent, forcing them into ever more restrictive areas. By adding a series of dummy tackles or jabs, you can often lead your opponent to commit a rash manoeuvre in an attempt to shake you off, often resulting in him or her losing momentary control of the ball. The timing of the tackle should hopefully coincide with the ball being slightly out of your opponent's control or in a weaker position. It is important to maintain a strong stick and ball contact, to resist the force of the opponent's momentum brushing aside your tackle.

(*PREVIOUS PAGE*) *Tackling with a flat stick: Having committed the attacker to one position, the defender has given himself the best possible chance of pulling off a successful tackle. The tackler sweeps the stick along the turf, using its full width to carry the ball beyond his opponent. Forearm strength, combined with power from the legs due to a low body position, will halt the momentum of the attacker, or at least leave him running on but dispossessed of the ball.*

(*RIGHT*) *Tackling on the open side: Jon Potter of England and Great Britain has forced the Indian winger to try and run round his open side. While matching the forward for speed, Jon runs with the player waiting for a slight loss of control, and then presents his open-side stick to the ball, carrying it past the opponent. As with many of the skills of hockey, timing is a vital factor.*

Tackling on the Reverse Side

The reverse side tackle is particularly difficult for beginners because it involves a one-handed movement with the wrist twisted fully in an anti-clockwise direction. But if it is acknowledged as being difficult to execute you can be assured that the forward with the ball will be all the more keen to try and pass you on

The reverse stick tackle: Pleshacov of Russia demonstrates a fine sense of timing, combined with arm strength, in executing the reverse stick tackle. With the stick fully reversed, the ball is trapped against the turf. While the ball is held in this position, the attacker's momentum carries him on and past the tackle. The fine margins for error in this technique make this the most penalised skill in the game, and therefore one that merits that little extra practice.

your left-hand side and gain some advantage from the fact that you may not have mastered the skill. It follows, therefore, that this is one tackling skill that should be practised over and over again until you feel as comfortable with it as you do with any of the other skills in your repertoire.

To be successful with this tackle you must twist the grip on your left hand so that the head or toe of the stick is pointing to the ground. The stick is then hooked over the ball and dragged away from the player in possession. Again it is important to adopt a low body position so that you can generate the maximum amount of strength for the tackle but – as with the tackle on the open side – you should be alongside your opponent to avoid the possibility of an infringement. The rules of hockey say that a player cannot interfere with an opponent's stick or body until contact with the ball has been established, so the risks of giving away a free hit in the high pressure atmosphere of a match are quite enormous unless you are quick enough on your feet and good enough with your timing.

With each tackle, the object should be to bring the ball away cleanly and set up a new opening for your own side. In a game like hockey, where speed is a vital factor, defence can be transformed into attack on the twist of a stick.

The Jab Tackle

This tackle is particularly effective on artificial surfaces because it enables the defender to use the springiness of the turf to give the ball that extra momentum to squeeze it out of the attacker's possession. It is a technique most often employed in tight situations, possibly around the circle, where the player with the ball is ducking and diving, trying to find that vital chink in the defence and create the opening for a shot on goal. The risks in this area of the field are highest because any infringement by the defending side is going to lead to a penalty corner, or even worse, a penalty stroke.

Generally the jab tackle is executed from a position side-on to the player with the ball. The idea is to get the head of the stick under the ball and then jab it away in your direction with a swift downward stabbing movement. If successful, the next movement will likely be a hit or push into one of the areas of safety to the side of the field. The jab tackle takes a lot of patient practice to perfect, and should be added to your armoury after the basic tackling techniques have been mastered. Some coaches encourage players to use the shadow technique to practise – that is, they stand them in sunlight or under floodlights on the training court and tell them to jab their shadow. This is a particularly effective way of getting a feel for the technique and its timing.

Fig. 22 (OVERLEAF) *The jab tackle: This move is often likened to the action of a fencer stabbing the ball. With one foot forward and the stick held in two hands, the tackler stalks his or her opponent, 'closing down' the gap. The tackler feints a series of dummy tackles, hoping to force the attacker into an error or loss of concentration. At that moment, the tackler jabs at the ball, often lifting it just over the opponent's stick and out of their control.*

The jab tackle: Ric Charlesworth of Australia demonstrates a high level of concentration, together with balanced body position, as he prepares to jab tackle. With legs astride but one foot forward, he stalks his opponent waiting for a moment's loss of control before stabbing the ball.

Laying Down the Stick

This is a technique which has become increasingly used in recent years particularly since the advent of the artificial playing surface. It requires a combination of fine timing and considerable strength as the stick has to be slammed into the ground in front of the advancing forward, and then held there with one arm outstretched to trap the ball firmly enough to force your opponent's momentum to carry him beyond you. Sean Kerly is a player who uses this tackle to tremendous effect but at the same time he has paid quite a price for his expertise. The fingers of his stick hand are badly gnarled from years of slamming his knuckles either into the abrasive surface of sand-filled Astro Turf, or onto the unforgiving boards of the indoor hockey court. Many players wear some form of finger protection, however, and don't incur such damage. Sean is philosophical and says he no longer needs it.

Laying down the stick: Sean Kerly of England and Great Britain demonstrates his defensive qualities. By presenting his stick horizontally, as for the reverse stick stop, he uses his strength to hold the ball wedged against the turf while the Belgian forward runs past dispossessed. Wrist and forearm strength, combined with cast-iron knuckles, make this 'long barrier' a particularly effective method of tackling on the reverse side.

The Diving Tackle

This is a manoeuvre I thought about long and hard before including it in the book. It is a desperate measure and not one that should be encouraged in young or inexperienced players trying to master the basic skills of the game. However, it is a tackle seen occasionally on the international stage, where it is sometimes pulled off with spectacular success, but often results in the defender spread-eagled with stick outstretched and the forward beyond him with acres of space (see picture of Ric Charlesworth page 66). This particular tackle should only be used when there is no other way of reaching the ball and no team-mate in a position to intercept the player with the ball. You should try to get as close to the attacker as possible and then lunge at the ball. All you can really expect to do under these circumstances is to push the ball out of the other player's possession and into an area of less danger.

Stefan Blocher of West Germany, one of the most spectacular exponents of the Indian dribble. Having cornered the ball around and wide of his opponent, he cuts back to leave the defender floundering.

Ric Charlesworth of Australia demonstrates his utter commitment to winning the ball by throwing himself full length to try and rob Volker Freid of West Germany.

Sean Kerly, seemingly marked with no room to spare, nevertheless shoots the ball with devastating effect, giving England victory over New Zealand in their World Cup pool match.

Shahid of India bemuses the Spanish defence in their World Cup match in London, 1986. The Spanish goalkeeper, however, moves quickly off his line to smother the oncoming forward before he has had time to take advantage of a potential dangerous situation.

Above: West Germany's Stefan Blocher attacks the Australian circle, while the defence musters depth and cover in numbers to try and stop him.
Below: Hasan Sadar of Pakistan weaves his way through the Australian defence in the 1984 Olympic semi-final, to secure his side's victory.

The save which won Britain their place in the Olympic semi finals – was it reflex action or did the author know exactly where it was going? You will have to make up your own mind. The penalty stroke-taker is Ties Kruize of Holland, one of the game's all-time greats, who has won medals at every stage from club to country. Also a former European Superstar, his arm and wrist strength give him the ability to flick and hit the ball with tremendous power.

Imran Sherwani of England – one of hockey's most incisive forwards – attacks the Australian defence during the World Cup final of 1986. John Bestall, the Australian full-back, tackles with a low, strong jab tackle.

GOALSCORING

Without apologising for stating the obvious, success at the game of hockey will always come down to scoring more goals than the opposition. Your team might have the best defence in its league but if the forwards are not doing their bit and are failing to score goals at the other end, then you'll never win your share of trophies.

Strangely enough, and vital though it is, goalscoring is a skill sadly neglected by the majority of club squads. Many coaches are prepared to put hours of time and effort into the other skills of the game, yet at the same time seem to believe that goalscoring is an instinctive talent that can be left to take care of itself.

Naturally, instinct does play a part – the ability to slip into the right position at the right time will always set apart the 'natural goalscorer' from his or her less gifted team-mates. Having said that, however, the skills involved in shooting at goal can be developed and fine-tuned and should therefore be practised regularly by players of all standards.

Hockey is a fast, physically demanding game and generally where teams are evenly matched, goalscoring opportunities are few and far between. The target is small and responsibility for hitting it will often be down to one or two members of the team. Their success or failure will inevitably influence the outcome of the match and therefore those players who have demonstrated the ability to find the net regularly will invariably be lauded as the stars of the team.

Goals are the objective of the game and, for the most part, are the reason why spectators are attracted to a match. Even as a goalkeeper, I must concede that the most exciting sight in hockey is seeing the ball flash inch-perfect through that most miniscule of gaps and into the net – hopefully the opposition's!

Good goalscorers come in a variety of shapes, sizes and styles, yet it is readily apparent that there are a number of common strands which single out these players from the rest of the pack. They will always have the ability to hit the ball very hard and an eye for placing it accurately at a target often measured in inches rather than feet, but more importantly the successful goalscorers will be those players who have the sense to know just when to move and which position offers them the optimum advantage.

A soccer analogy is appropriate here, in so far as the good striker – like the good goalscorer – is the player who best exploits the space behind or beyond the defender as the ball is played in. Such players always seem to have an acre of space when they receive the ball. Under match pressure, of course, space is converted into time and time enables the forward to choose his spot and outfox the exposed goalkeeper.

Natural talent will always be a significant factor in the consistent goalscorer but that apart, there are many skills that can be groomed and honed by regular

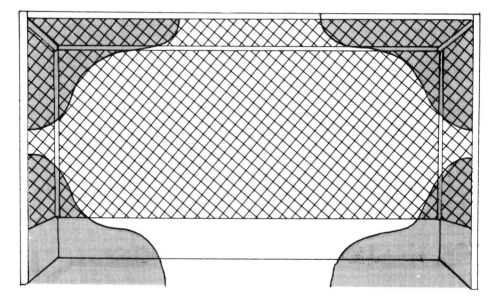

Fig 23 *Areas of Goal: The effective goalscorer carries a mental image of the goal, aiming for the primary targets (the four corners shown in the diagram). These are the areas least likely to be effectively covered by the goalkeeper. When lining up to shoot, however, the striker should also instantaneously evaluate the goalkeeper's understanding of angles, the style he adopts and any particular technique he uses, such as smothering the ball. According to the shooting position adopted, some of the primary targets will be more penetrable than others (the far post is generally the easier target). However, a little guile and deception can often create a whole variety of angles to shoot at.*

(RIGHT) Good footwork is no footwork: Sean Kerly demonstrates that opportunities in front of goal rarely occur in text-book situations. If the ball presents itself, the shot must be executed with power and accuracy, irrespective of the position of the feet and interference from the defender – who will use any means to try and disrupt the shooter.

and intense practice, preferably under match-play conditions. Too many players seem to believe that they can merely stand towards the top of the circle firing stationary balls at the goal and use their success rate at this exercise as a benchmark for their performance in competition.

In hockey – as with so many other fast-moving team games – the striker often shoots blind and from instinct. The goal becomes but a mental image, a picture in the mind that represents the target and includes each of the encroaching defenders. This instinctive positioning comes as a result of a combination of much painstaking practice and genuine natural talent. The Great Britain forward, Sean Kerly, is the envy of all because of this very quality. And besides consistently putting himself in the right position at the right time, Sean demonstrates an ability to make the best use of his shot regardless of the position of the ball in relation to his feet. There is a saying in hockey that good footwork is no footwork, and Sean is living confirmation of this. Watching him in action you will soon learn that he can hit, flick, push or deflect the ball in the direction of goal without any regard to the position of his body.

The top Australian forwards are other good examples. They manoeuvre their bodies into the best position for the stroke regardless of whether this entails a

headlong dive into the thick of the action. Scoring goals is often the result of the striker doing anything but the conventional move – this being the key to the element of surprise that ensures the goal attempt is successful.

Goalscoring opportunities seldom present themselves from textbook angles, so it follows that the best strikers are those players who have an ability to improvise, deceiving defenders and goalkeepers with lightning attempts on goal from the most improbable angles. One of the most effective ploys is the deflection caused by the forward putting a firmly held stick in the path of the ball, and using its momentum to change the angle of the ball. In this movement the stick is often dropped horizontal onto the ground to offer the largest possible surface area. Alternatively, the head of the stick can be jabbed firmly into the line of the approaching ball and the deflection executed this way.

It will certainly take a good deal of practice to perfect this particular skill because establishing the correct angle of intervention is critical. Ideally the head should be in line with both the stick and the ball, but more importantly the skill should only be attempted under the right circumstances. Its effectiveness is governed by the speed at which the original cross is played, so it follows that wing crosses, free hits and long corners are the most likely.

It will always be rare for a forward to enter the 'D' in full control of the ball and with sufficient time to choose a spot and take a shot. It is therefore essential that a forward has the ability to improvise the hitting and flicking strokes to produce that final shot on goal. The slap hit – where the hit and the flick are combined – is particularly suitable for use in goalscoring attempts because it enables the ball to be propelled quickly and accurately. Similarly, the shortened grip – where the top hand is brought down to the lower hand and a more wristy action created – is also effective.

Once the basic strokes have been mastered, it will always be the question of improvisation which separates the consistent goalscorer from the rest. The introduction of artificial surfaces has also brought about a whole range of new strokes made possible because the hockey pitch is now both true and springy. One favourite is the drag-flick which can be used to devastating effect both from short range and on the run. Here the ball is either received behind the line of the body, or left there by the shooter if already under control. The technique then is to drag the ball forward rapidly past the body line and then turn the drag movement into either a push or a flick at the most opportune time – usually when the goalkeeper is committed and therefore wrong-footed. The key to success with this stroke is to keep the ball accelerating forward and yourself in control of the final movement.

Chipping and squeezing the ball have also become more possible because of plastic surfaces and these manoeuvres are particularly effective when it comes to clearing a prostrate goalkeeper. Reverse-stick flicking and scooping also enable the forward to get a shot in quickly and accurately.

On those ideal occasions when the forward does break clear and get into the circle with the ball under full control, the final outcome should be a goal. In reality, however, the situation is often very different. Even the most accom-

Fig. 24 *Deflecting with the jab technique: By utilising the speed of the cross, it is possible simply to deflect the ball into the goal. Both the upright jabbing technique (a), where the stick is thrust through the line of the ball, and the laying down technique (b), can be used with equal effect on the open or reverse sides (depending on the situation and position around goal). In deflection goals, the attacker should aim for the 'near post' to allow for the ball being carried on by its momentum.*

plished players can find themselves panicked into rushing their shot and placing it badly. It is vital to maintain complete control of the situation if the move is to finish with a goal. There are three crucial elements involved in this. The first is to commit the defender or goalkeeper to making the first move. The second involves moving the ball into space. Thirdly – and with all speed – is the shot, executed by means of the most suitable stroke available. Feints and dummies are often used to commit the opponent and create space for the shot.

The rules of hockey – unlike most other ball games – do not allow the goalkeeper to catch and hold the ball, so in the event of a shot on goal not hitting the

The 'one on one': Having committed the Dutch goalkeeper at the top of the circle, Stephen Batchelor of England and Great Britain demonstrates speed and control to create a goalscoring opportunity in this World Cup match (1986). 'One on one' opportunities are few and far between, and the attacker must know exactly what he or she is trying to achieve stage by stage, if a goal is to be the result.

back of the net then the most likely outcome will be some sort of rebound. Forwards should always be aware of this, taking mental note of the angles and getting into position to take advantage. Naturally, practice plays a significant part in learning to read this particular aspect of the game.

As I mentioned at the outset, scoring goals is the objective of the game so in this context I find it astonishing that many coaches devote so little time to this particular skill. In club houses the world over you will find players bemoaning the fact that their side enjoyed all the play but failed to take their chances in front of goal. The solution is in their own hands. They must practise the skill over and over and wherever possible re-create match-play conditions where the sticks and the bodies are flying and the shooting opportunities timed in micro-seconds. Goalscoring is a talent, and regular goalscoring comes from a combination of instinct and timing. As the game develops, so do the expectations of the spec-

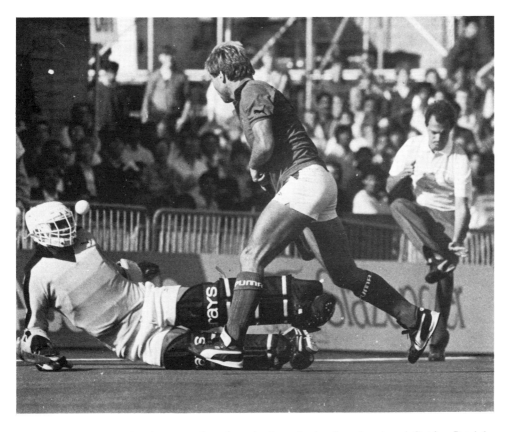

A very large percentage of goals are scored not from the direct shot but from the rebound. Stephen Batchelor 'reads' the rebound of the ball off the goalkeeper and prepares to volley in the half chance, despite umpire Deo having penalised an earlier infringement against the Pakistan goalkeeper. Positioning is the all-important factor, and practice at match-like situations will put the attacker in the right place at the right time.

tators. The goalscorers are the heroes of the game and as such carry an enormous responsibility on their shoulders. Players like Sean Kerly deserve every bit of the praise that is heaped upon them.

Goalscoring: Having shrugged off the close attentions of the New Zealand defender, Sean Kerly pounces onto the ball to create another goalscoring opportunity. Watching Sean in action, you will see that he trains as he plays, creating and taking chances that many forwards would not even consider.

The key points to remember from this chapter are as follows:

• Goalscoring is essentially about preparation and anticipation;

• Try to create a mental map of the goal position in relation to your own position in the circle;

• Successful scoring can depend on your ability to produce a shot of power and accuracy, irrespective of your feet position;

• Do not swerve from your determination to put the ball in the back of the net, whatever the obstacle.

GOALKEEPING

The goalkeeper is a vital member of any hockey team. Often it is a good performance or, indeed, a faulty one which makes the difference between victory and
defeat. It is a position where technique is at a premium, and let me dismiss one
myth from the outset by telling you that in my view there is really no such thing
as a natural when it comes to hockey goalkeeping. Those players who achieve
success and recognition in this position – and I accept that some do earn the
accolade 'natural' from the fans – do so through a long and painstaking development of their technique.

Hockey goalkeeping has become something of a science in recent years and
anyone who has observed this particular position closely during an international
tournament will have seen that there is really no single, generally accepted style.
Everything about the goalkeeper's skill evolves from the individual interpretation
of a number of common factors.

The goalkeeper is reckoned to have no less than sixteen primary functions and
responsibilities, and when you acknowledge that only one of these is to stop
shots on goal, you will appreciate just how crucial a player he has become.
That final shot is often merely the end result of several other factors of the
goalkeeper's game and it is these other skills which are most often neglected,
particularly when it comes to teaching or coaching the position.

Any goalkeeper worth his position in a team should demonstrate an ability to
dominate or even rule events in his or her circle or 'D'.

Remember, this is the one position where the player is allowed to use his
hands, feet and body to play the ball and, more importantly, it is the one part of
the field where the attacking player will be hoping to turn his side's territorial
advantage into a goal.

By a series of clear, precise instructions the goalkeeper should be able to organise the structure of his defence. In reality, these organisational skills extend beyond the circle because the goalkeeper's strategic position enables him to observe the entire defensive picture. The ability to 'read' the game is therefore one of the most important qualities that a goalkeeper must develop. Unfortunately, this turns out to be one of the few skills which is almost impossible to coach successfully. The best contribution that the coach can hope to make is by organising a variety of match-play situations on the training field and in doing so allow the goalkeeper to experience dealing with each of them in turn. Experience is such a vital factor in goalkeeping, it's no wonder that goalkeepers – whether their game is hockey, soccer or whatever – often reach their peak towards the end of their playing careers.

Equipment

A hockey ball hit with serious intent can often be travelling at speeds in excess of 100 mph when it reaches the goalkeeper. When you bear in mind the distance from which it is shot, you will understand just how important it is for the player on the receiving end to be wearing the right equipment. Anyone responsible for teaching, coaching or introducing young players to the game should be mindful of the need for good quality equipment. The eventual introduction of approved gear and formal safety standards should go a long way towards eliminating weak equipment which could permit pain or even serious injury.

Pads and kickers should be strong enough to ensure that although the goalkeeper may feel the ball on contact, it is not a feeling of pain. Cricket pads, I should stress, are not suitable. Coaches of young players should appreciate that if a youngster feels pain from the ball during his formative training sessions, he'll more than likely soon go off the idea of becoming a full-time 'keeper.

After the leg and foot protection should come padding for the soft tissue organs of the abdomen. Gloves and gauntlets should be constructed in such a way as to prevent breakages and should have enough padding to ensure that the player feels comfortable stopping a fast shot without the fear of pain.

One of the most important recent developments has been the helmet. Artificial surfaces have greatly increased the speed of the ball, and it is my considered opinion that no goalkeeper should take to the field these days without the protection of a proper helmet designed for hockey. I find it staggering that some players are still taking to the field in skate-boarding helmets, or even face masks, which give no head protection and often shatter on impact. I would suggest that any player taking up the position of goalkeeper should wear a proper helmet from day one. That way it will quickly become second nature and require no adjusting to at a later stage.

Ice hockey-type shorts and chest pads are becoming increasingly popular when it comes to carrying out certain techniques. Again these should be worn as early as possible so that the junior player feels comfortable wearing them when he begins to develop the more advanced skills involved in sliding and smothering the ball.

Goalkeeping equipment: It is essential that young goalkeepers have confidence in the protection of their equipment from the outset. Investing in good quality kickers, pads, abdominal box, gloves and helmet will allow the goalkeeper to concentrate on the skills of the game, rather than any pain.

The Leg and Feet Skills

As with any outfield player, the goalkeeper must be equally mindful of the position of his head. Body control and movement – whether in a considered action or a reaction save – are both controlled from the head, and faults in technique can often be quickly traced back to this basic flaw.

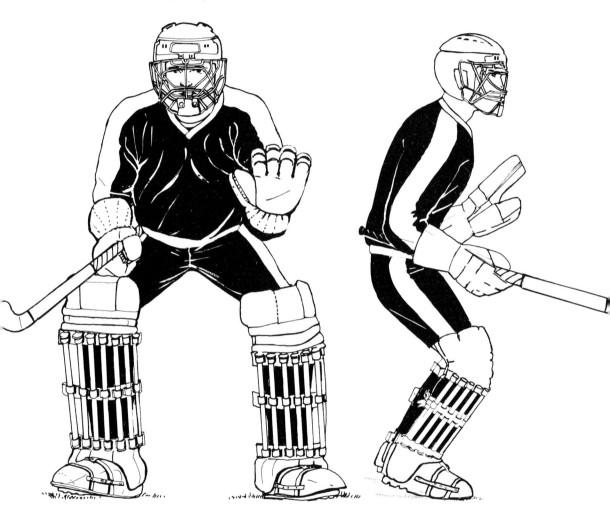

Fig. 25 *The basic stance: Depending on physique and style, the basic stance (shown here from the front and side) may vary from goalkeeper to goalkeeper. However, the chin-above-knees-above-toes position, with the heels off the ground, remains essential, and faults in this basic stance lie at the cause of many of the failures in technique that can develop later on. The position of the hands and stick may vary slightly for comfort, but they should always be where they can move as quickly and smoothly as possible to save the shot.*

Beyond the head, there is a basic stance for all goalkeeping movements. The knees should be slightly bent and the back crouched with the head forward, with the chin above the knees and the knees above the toes. The goalkeeper should be relaxed yet alert. Some players find the head position difficult to achieve at first because it seems an unnatural stance to adopt, particularly because any exaggeration would cause the 'keeper to overbalance and pitch forward! In many goalkeepers, however, the temptation is to carry the head too far back. This has the effect of causing the ball to ricochet up into the air on impact, with the associated danger of it flying loose and therefore possibly into the possession of an opponent. At the same time the sudden change in body angle will most often pitch the goalkeeper backwards and onto the ground, leaving him hopelessly exposed and unable to deal with any follow-up scoring attempt. One of the first rules of goalkeeping, therefore, is to take all the time necessary to get the head position right and to feel comfortable with it.

When shaping up to a shot at the feet or legs, the goalkeeper's instinct must tell him to do one of two things. He must either control or trap the ball, or use the power of the shot to direct the rebound elsewhere. If he chooses the first option it is important to get the head behind the line of the ball, then use the foot or leg to absorb the momentum before clearing to safety with the foot or stick. However, it is more likely these days that the goalkeeper will, whenever possible, adopt the save-clear technique. This is a technique developed by me some years ago and now universally adopted by goalkeepers of all standards. If executed properly, it has the advantage of enabling the ball to be saved, then played well clear of the danger area, all in one smooth sweeping movement. Again, it is a skill which requires good head positioning and precise timing. As the shot is fired in, the goalkeeper shapes up and then plays his foot or leg through the line of the ball with the aim of making contact at a point just in front of the line of the body. It should be emphasised that there is a clear difference between kicking the ball – which requires leaving the weight over the back foot – and the save-clear technique which requires the body weight to be pivoted in favour of the saving leg (see fig. 27, page 88). Many goalkeepers adopting this technique tend to save the ball when it is level with the line of the body and this often results in poor rebound power and control. Making contact to the front of the body-line is the only way to achieve the momentum needed to make this skill effective. Once the save-clear manoeuvre has been completed, it is important for the goalkeeper to bring the back leg up level with the front, regaining a secondary balanced position should the ball not reach the intended area of safety and instead fall into the opposition's possession. By quickly regaining position, the goalkeeper should be well placed to deal with any subsequent shot.

Angles are vitally important to a goalkeeper and, wherever possible, skills should be practised in a full-sized goal in order that an intuitive understanding of the goal in relation to every position within the 'D' can be developed. Knowing whether a shot is on goal or wide without having to look around is crucial if a reasonable standard of play is to be achieved.

The beginner should start by imagining a smaller 'D' within the existing one about three to four metres in diameter from the goal-line, although the actual dimensions should be governed by the reaction time and reach of the player concerned. This position is achieved by drawing a mental line between the striker and the centre of the goal and, if calculated correctly, the positioning of the 'keeper should reduce the amount of goal that the striker can shoot at. Spectators who take the view that 'the forward keeps hitting the goalkeeper with his shots' are wrong. They should understand that they're watching a goalkeeper playing well and covering all the angles properly.

(BELOW) The save and clear: This sequence shows a perfect demonstration of balance and timing. The goalkeeper absorbs the power of the shot, killing it almost dead, and then adjusts the position of his feet in relation to the ball so that the clearance is made to safety to the sides, away from the onrushing forwards. Notice how the head and body weight are forward, maintaining the balance and smoothness of action.

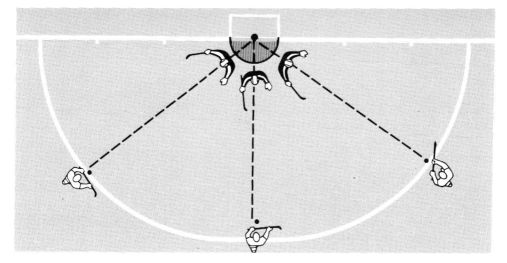

Fig. 26 *The 'D' position around goal: The goalkeeper's basic position can be illustrated by drawing an imaginary 'D' some three of four metres in radius from the centre of the goal. The optimum position is achieved by taking stance on the edge of this 'D', on line between the centre of the goal and the ball.*

Fig. 27 *The save-clear technique with the secondary position: Having made the decision to use the 'save-clear' technique, the goalkeeper leads the movement with his head, driving through the line of the ball in front of the body line and turning the boot to give the required angle of rebound (a). The trailing leg is then brought up to the saving leg so that a secondary saving position is achieved, facing the correct angle for any follow-up rebound shot. Power for this technique is supplied by the back leg, while the leading head and arms provide a smooth and balanced movement.*

Clearing the Ball

The hockey goalkeeper has the advantage of being able to use legs and feet to stop the ball and/or effect a clearance. Naturally the stick is also available, but to save the ball with the leg or foot and then use the stick to either push or flick it clear, is a manoeuvre likely to consume valuable time. There are a number of ways to get the ball away: it can be kicked first time with the instep for an accurate but less powerful clearance, or it can be blasted away with the top of the foot, sacrificing accuracy for power. In either case the goalkeeper must first and foremost be mindful of safety. Generally, clearances should be directed to the sides of the field, i.e. the areas of least danger. However, with experience, it should be possible to kick clearances safely through the ranks of advancing forwards and to the stick of a retreating team-mate. Safety, though, must remain the primary objective and a hard kick to the touchlines, although less spectacular, will always be better than the mis-timed placed clearance that ends up right at the stick of an opponent in a position to pick up the ball and score.

Kicking the ball in the air: Many goalkeepers are penalised for dangerously kicking a clearance in the air. During the 1986 World Cup the author clears a volley with power, but wide of the onrushing Pakistan forward. Even with a powerful kick such as this, it is essential to maintain a smooth approach, clear mental image of one's intentions and a good follow-through if the clearance is to be successful.

Fig. 28 *Clearing to the side: The onrushing forwards (A and B) are preventing the goalkeeper from simply playing the ball forward to a team-mate. The goalkeeper therefore kicks the ball beyond the reach of the opponents, away from the goal to the sidelines.*

I try to discourage use of the toe punt (kicking front-on with the foot) because I feel strongly that it is not to be recommended as a means of clearance. This is because it requires kicking across the line of the ball and, more often than not, results in a mis-kick.

It should now be clear to any aspiring goalkeeper that a good kicking action with either foot is vital. The skill should be practised frequently, either with a hockey ball on the field or a tennis ball in the back yard. The technique is broadly similar to soccer and the same basic rules apply. The ball may lift if the head isn't properly over it, or lack power because the follow through is weak. Every goalkeeper's objective should be to achieve the same skills with a hockey ball as they would wish to do with a football.

Saves with the Hand or Stick

In essence, the stick should be considered an extension of the hand and as such be able to cover a greater area to the goalkeeper's right side. In the many cases of poor hand and stick saves, the majority are the result of the goalkeeper snatching at the ball rather than taking it in. The diagram opposite shows how, from a well balanced position, the goalkeeper can cover most if not all of the goal, even from the goal line. The goalkeeper can be even more effective by advancing towards the point of shot, thus narrowing the shooter's angle.

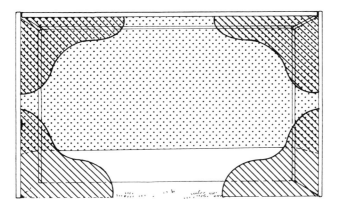

Fig. 29 *Areas of goal: The goalkeeper should in theory be able to cover a very large area of the goal. If the goalkeeper shows sufficient proficiency in the basic goalkeeping techniques, the striker will be forced to aim for the small areas which remain (those diagonally shaded above).*

Usually, the goalkeeper will use the palm of the hand or stick to absorb some of the power from the shot, and to redirect the ball either vertically down to the ground for clearance with the stick or foot, or alternatively around the upright or over the bar to concede a long corner. The power of the shot and position of the goalkeeper's body will be the deciding factors. The secret of this manoeuvre, as with so many others already described, is to keep the eye on the ball at all times.

Fig. 30 *Saving with the stick: The principles for saving with the stick or hand are broadly similar, with the stick being considered an extension of the hand. Whether the goalkeeper's intention is to stop the ball dead or use the power of the shot to deflect the ball over or round the post, a leading movement of the head combined with a smooth action will produce a much improved success rate at this skill.*

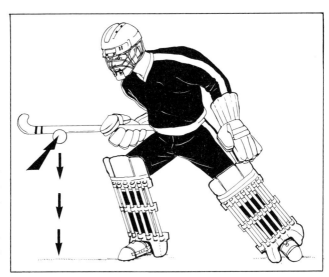

Smothering or Spreading – Taking the Ball off an Attacker

Whether the goalkeeper is taking the ball off an encroaching opponent, rushing to smother a shot, or laying down at a corner, the principle remains the same: create the largest horizontal barrier possible.

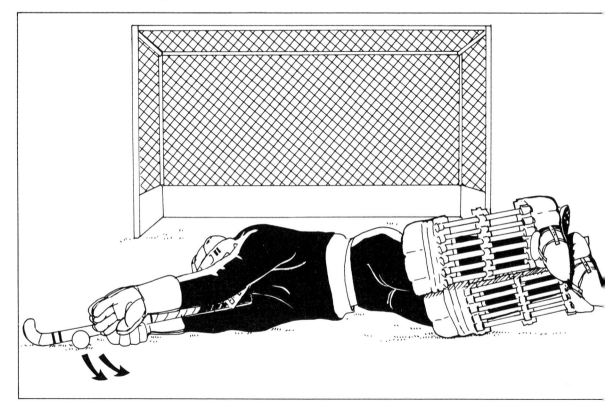

Fig. 31 *Smothering or spreading: The techniques of smothering or spreading rely on covering as large a horizontal surface area as possible. By timing the presentation of this long barrier, the goalkeeper can leave the attacker with no room for manoeuvre and force him to overtake the ball as the goalkeeper engulfs it. The use of the stick as an extension of this barrier, and as a method of clearance whilst prostrate, should be regularly practised, as to miss the ball often leaves the goalkeeper stranded and helpless.*

By correct positioning it is possible to force a forward to take the side you most want him to, although this can be difficult because forwards are much more mobile on the increasingly popular artificial surfaces. As with tackling, the key to success in this particular discipline is timing – choosing the most effective moment in which to smother the ball. You must close down the gap at the top of the 'D' then, as the attacker attempts to penetrate the circle, spread your body, presenting a long horizontal barrier. Should the player still get beyond the line of the head, use the stick to sweep the ball away. Remember, a smooth controlled

Smothering an opponent in possession: The Dutch goalkeeper 'takes no prisoners' as he slides his horizontal barrier through the New Zealand attacker in their World Cup pool match (1986). With the goalkeeper having taken the ball through the line of play, the attacker has become airborne due to the 'keeper's momentum. You have to expect a little knock occasionally in a fast game such as hockey!

action is far more effective than a mad charge which is easy to pass. Assuming the tackle is successful, it is vital for the goalkeeper to regain his or her feet quickly, ready to repel the next attack.

Successful goalkeeping is very much a combination of experience and mental imagery. Each and every goalkeeper will have his or her own blend of techniques developed from hours of practice and, wherever possible, this practice should simulate actual match conditions and the pressures that go with it. Only by putting yourself under constant pressure will you reach the stage where the moves all become second nature and you are operating on instinct rather than active thought.

Once this position has been achieved, the long hard road to perfection begins. From now on you will be using this store of technical know-how in a variety of situations, combining and modifying these skills as the situation demands and adopting improvisations in the fractions of seconds available when the unexpected happens.

All players make mistakes but it is often the goalkeeper who carries the ultimate responsibility because a mistake by a player in this position will almost inevitably lead to a goal from the opposition. It goes without saying that the goalkeepers must have absolute confidence in their own abilities to do the job in hand, but ultimately they do shoulder a greater responsibility because they must transmit their own confidence to the players around them. Perhaps equally importantly, the goalkeeper must exude confidence to the opposition because there is nothing better than a group of forwards who are in awe of the opposition's 'keeper. When they get their scoring opportunities they will always hesitate for that vital moment, perhaps to try and pick their spot, perhaps to decide whether to hit the ball or flick it. Nine times out of ten it is the opening you have been waiting for, and you can be off your line to smother the shot or adjust your position to close off the greater part of the goal.

Inevitably there will be errors, but you must try not to let it affect your game. Make a mental note for later consideration by all means, but on the day put the moment to the back of your mind and don't brood about it. It's important to take such things in your stride and get on with the game.

It is generally accepted that the people who achieve in sport are almost always those who have carefully mapped-out objectives, be they in the short-, medium- or long-term. Goalkeeping is no exception, whether the 'keeper is fifteen or fifty and playing for a club fifth eleven or their country. Whatever style of goalkeeper you feel you are or indeed wish to become, working within a disciplined pattern will always help you. My own motto has always been that if you play only as well as you did in the previous match you are depreciating as a goalkeeper.

Goalkeepers, like goalscorers, are the focal point of the game, individuals whose actions are most closely scrutinised and successes or failures carefully chronicled. Failure in both positions can ruin your weekend; success and the satisfaction of a good performance can leave you with a warm glow and the feeling that your job on the field is without doubt the most rewarding of all.

The author saves Terry Walsh's goal attempt during the Champions Trophy in Perth, 1983.

Points to bear in mind when goalkeeping are as follows:

• Adopt a balanced body position, with the head well forward, for all manoeuvres;

• Keep a clear mental image of your body position, angles and intentions;

• Maintain a strong and determined domination and control of your circle.

TEAM AND GROUP PLAY

Hockey is a team game and it is the mix of individual skills in group action rather than the talents of one or two players that produces fluid, successful play from the unit as a whole.

The importance of co-ordinated team play cannot be over-emphasised. There are many teams worldwide who – despite being packed with highly skilled individuals – still lose regularly to teams with lesser individual ability but greater cohesion. Once players new to the game have mastered the basics, it is important for them to get into an organised squad and begin working towards that balanced blend.

As with so many things, there is no one specific area which can be readily identified as the key to successful team play. Coaches down the years have all been striving to discover the same secret, but I can assure you that this so-called magic formula just doesn't exist. However, it is possible to analyse the play of those teams which achieve consistent success and identify key areas of their collective discipline which contribute to setting them apart from the also-rans. I intend to devote some space to styles of play and tactical patterns in the next chapter, but here we will concentrate on the interaction between two players, or between groups of players, and the ways in which they communicate. Body language – the signs, sounds and signals that pass between players – is as important in hockey as in many other team sports.

The ability to co-ordinate action with an understanding of what is going on in the immediate vicinity is known as 'scanning'. It is a valuable skill, yet too often it is one aspect of the game that attracts scant attention from players of varying levels of ability – a fact amply illustrated by the player who consistently looks better in practice than he does under match conditions. The ability to look up and take in as complete a picture as possible is a vital skill in the armoury of the top class player. It doesn't matter whether you're in possession of the ball, marking, taking up position or trying to create a goalscoring opportunity – the importance of taking in the entire picture cannot be over-emphasised. It is a skill which should be practised regularly and in groups to simulate as far as possible real match-play conditions.

The skill itself often requires a slight lifting of the head which can have the effect of introducing a bobbing movement into the player's action. The best way to eliminate this is by adopting a more upright position.

Scanning can be divided into two separate skills: the near or close scan, where the player observes the movements of players and developments in play close by him, and the long-distance scan, where the player takes in the entire field before him. So important is scanning that one widely held theory purports that a player's position within the team may ultimately be decided on his scanning ability. Clearly, it is successful scanning that enables many of the world's top players to demonstrate vision in seeing passes or anticipating movements that vital moment before their opponents.

The Sounds and Signals of Hockey

Good communication between players helps create a cohesive unit in all team sports and hockey is of course no exception. The type of communication and response depends on the area of the field or the proximity of team-mates, but hockey is certainly not a quiet game – advice, comment and gesticulation are in plentiful supply throughout each match. Needless to say, the advice and complaints should be confined to team-mates and never take in the umpire.

Coaches often overlook the importance of talking, particularly when dealing with youngsters who are still in the early stages of learning the game. In fact this is the right place to start drilling into the novice that members of the team must help one another in every way possible. This help should include pointing out both the dangers and the opportunities if you think your team-mate is unaware of them. Controlled comment from a team-mate is an invaluable asset in assessing situations and, particularly when in possession, well-evaluated calling helps the player with the ball to decide whether a particular pass is on or not.

Naturally, experience plays a big part in developing these non-physical aspects of the game and only full-scale practice sessions and frank post-match feedback will help a player decide whether, on some occasions, he might be offering not enough information or indeed – as has been the case with me from time to time – too much!

When a team has been playing together for some time, there is a danger that opponents will begin reading the lines of communication and anticipating the projected movements. At this stage code words and phrases are often introduced. However, this is very much a refinement of the skill and not something the beginner should be unduly concerned with. It is only at the higher levels of the game, where teams study their opponents in detail before every meeting, that these potential chinks will occur. During the learning and intermediate stages, good on-field communication, which leads to cohesive team-play, should be enough to see off most other teams.

Silent communication can be just as effective as shouting in many on-field situations. Very often when a player is beyond his opponent it is possible to signal by pointing the stick or nodding the head, or even by turning the head of the stick from left to right and vice-versa. Again, however, this form of communication only develops through understanding, practice and feedback among the players concerned.

Games can be won and lost by good or bad communication and there is no doubt that the coach who underestimates its importance is sending his or her team out at a disadvantage.

Reading the Game

This is probably the most important perceptual skill, and it can be broken down into three parts to make up what is generally accepted as selective attention. In hockey, the honing of this ability is vital due to the speed of the game. Selective attention can be divided thus:

1. Understanding the critical cues;

2. Recognising these cues when they occur;

3. Locking onto them to the exclusion of everything else.

The player who has successfully mastered these skills is the one who appears 'cool' and with time to spare on the field, the player whom spectators in the crowd describe as 'faultless' and 'a class above the rest'. Reading the game is like being at the scene of a crime: the clues are there for all to see, but only the good reader – like the good detective – picks up on them and follows them through. There is an element of instinct about reading the game but even assuming that this basic quality is present, any player who wants to obtain the most personal satisfaction from his or her hockey will have to work hard at building up his or her perception.

Defence and Attack as a Group

Team play in the game of hockey revolves around three basic objectives:

1. To construct attacking moves to create goalscoring opportunities;

2. To prevent the opposition from mounting and sustaining attacks;

3. To maintain a high level of possession so as to achieve objectives 1 and 2.

It is no coincidence that the consistently successful teams of recent years have not only developed high levels of team work, but have also had particularly effective defensive strategies. In reality, the transformation from a defensive position into an attacking one is not that great. Remember the old cliché, 'Attack is the best form of defence'? It's right because it is the interaction between forward and defensive players and their ability to link over the length of the field that create problems for the opposition.

The essence of defensive control is a perfect understanding of cover and marking responsibilities among all eleven players, enabling each one to play his or her own key role as part of the overall unit. The stature of a team can often be measured by the amount of discipline its players demonstrate in keeping to these responsibilities as the opposition put them under pressure around their own goal. It is vital that players keep a cool head in this situation. Authoritative control must be maintained, although that doesn't mean there won't still be a place for a mixture of adrenalin and courage when it comes to keeping the opposition out.

Naturally, systems of play will influence the roles of some players, just as changes in the laws of the game (the offside law for instance) will affect others. However the rules may change, though, a good reading of angles, and therefore good position in relation to your team-mates, will always remain of paramount importance. Ideally, the covering player should take up a position about 40 degrees to the side of his team-mate and about eight metres behind when the play is close (but obviously further apart when the ball is further away). The triangle thus formed deprives the player with the ball of space and therefore offers most cover to the defenders as they take up new positions.

All eleven players must get involved in cover-play, which is an integral part of team work in the defensive formation. It is a skill which relies very much upon

Fig. 32 *Cover for the tackling player: By reducing the number of players, it is easier to understand the simple principles of defensive cover. The triangular formation created by B and C covering A gives support both to the sides and in depth. This considerably reduces not only the passing options of the attackers, but also the chances of the player in possession going alone. Sometimes this depth of cover is impossible, particularly out on the flanks; here the cover should be in-field, forcing the attacker to pass out to the wings.*

the ability of individuals within the team to read the game and anticipate moves correctly. Each member of the team is dependent on the movement of team-mates. At any given time there will be a number of competing options and it is here that good lines of communication help a team to make the right choice.

The immediate objective of the nearest defending player is to delay or hold up the opposition as much as possible. This might involve pushing the opposition out wide, interfering with the player in possession by getting a tackle in, or simply by being in the way. Any or all of these actions give the defensive team the time to reorganise and cut down the number of options available to the player with the ball.

The time gained can help other players take up new marking positions, although marking is a broad term describing a variety of actions, each dependent on a player's intentions. Good marking is a skill in itself, and it is often an extremely fine balance between being too close and too far away. Coaches are forever arguing over whether players should mark shoulder to shoulder or at a given distance and I'm afraid there is really no hard and fast rule. The decision has to be governed by any particular player's speed, strength and style of play. The objective of the marking player, however, is clear. He or she should be in a position to either intercept any ball intended for the opponent, or make a tackle as the ball is received and the other player is attempting to bring it under control. It follows that the nearer the ball is delivered to your opponent, the closer you – the defender – should be, without offering the option of a simple pass into space behind you which would enable the attacking player to run around you and leave you stranded.

If these rules have been followed and the team has tackled back, marked and covered the opposing attack as an integral unit, the chances are that you will have regained possession without conceding a goal and are ready to set up your own attack. Where possible the attack should be swift and direct but the style should vary to avoid predictability. Naturally, there will be times when an individual player might break for goal, but generally attacks should involve five, six or even more players, particularly if a side is taking advantage of the full width of the field. The more players used, the further the opposition will be stretched and the greater the chance of eventually creating a two-against-one advantage, and with it, a possible opening for a shot at goal.

Once an opposition attack has been broken down and possession regained, it is important that those players without the ball quickly manoeuvre themselves away from their own markers to give the person with the ball as many options as possible for launching the attacking movement. The player with the ball may decide to take on the defender closing in on him, but more likely a pass will turn out to be the safest option. Remember that the object is to keep possession until a scoring opportunity can be created! Usually a string of square passes will follow with a through ball forward each time a gap is exposed.

In my experience it has been the fault of many forwards to believe that their sole responsibility upon receiving the ball is to take on an opponent. They forget – or indeed ignore – the fact that a quick square pass, a turn and then a sprint into space for the through ball can leave the defender uncertain whether to follow the ball or stick with the opponent. Successfully executed, this can often create that vital breakthrough and go on to lead to a goal.

The importance of the support and involvement of as many members of the team as possible cannot be over-emphasised. Hockey, in common with most team games, is a simple affair where success relies on the control and possession of the ball. Far too many teams, though, give the ball away needlessly or speculate unnecessarily. Often, teams of similar capabilities are only separated by the superior way in which one side holds onto the ball.

The secret when in possession is to keep both ball and players moving. Hockey is a fast game and opposition weaknesses can be exploited by constantly switch-

From defence to attack as a group: Having robbed the Indian attackers of possession, Carsten Fischer of West Germany quickly counter-attacks in their World Cup (1986) pool match. Keller, the West German centre-back, keeps in close support for the square pass as the Indian forwards sprint back to set up their defensive cover, the nearest player committing for the tackle as the other players cover behind. Although running at high speed, Fischer shows smooth control and confidence in his attacking strategy.

ing the ball from player to player in a variety of patterns. Naturally, this approach will leave some players sprinting into gaps and offering the person with the ball options that are rejected, but it should never be forgotten that this unrewarded running is still every bit as vital to the build-up as the pass that eventually leads to a successful shot on goal.

The winning team is the unit of eleven players who are disciplined in defence and then incisive in attack.

West Germany, one of the most consistently successful teams in recent years, show the understanding and team co-ordination that is the basis of their game. Stefan Blocher, the German spearhead, attacks deep into the Russian defence (Champions Trophy, Amsterdam 1987). The German captain, Heiner Dopp, gives close support for the square pass, while Ekhard Schmidt-Opper sprints for the pass forward to give Blocher a full range of alternatives.

Points to remember from this chapter are as follows:

● Hockey is a team game, and it is the way in which the individual units 'key together' that makes a team successful;

● Pockets of players creating simple triangulations give the greatest number of both defensive and attacking options;

● Possession of the ball is nine-tenths of the game; do not give the possession away cheaply.

SYSTEMS AND SET PIECES

The ideal team would win everything – league, cups, tournaments, the lot – because its squad would be made up of every conceivable type of player. Some would have the stamina to sustain the rigours of the regular season; others with enviable big match temperaments would be drafted in to see the team through cup ties, and then there would be other players called upon mainly for tournaments when perhaps a particular tactical sequence might make the difference between winning and losing. Ideal maybe, but a fairy-tale just the same because in hockey, while every successful club squad must include players capable of all these skills, it is unrealistic to expect quality players taking part in an amateur game to stay loyal to one team in return for maybe just a handful of outings each season.

In view of this it is understandable that some teams excel in cup competitions while others are tournament specialists. Perhaps the point might be better explained by means of an example. A team might decide to play a match with the two free-running forwards because it has suitable players within its ranks. If it is a cup tie, the team may well win because the players themselves are quite capable of excelling over seventy minutes and the edge they offer their side is the difference between the two teams. However, should that match be merely part of a tournament, I would expect the final outcome to be very different. The amount of running that these players would have to do in just one game would be so debilitating that they could never hope to maintain their fitness levels over the course of an entire tournament.

The aim of this chapter, therefore, is not to put forward the 'perfect system' – one that all teams can play to – but to discuss some of the advantages and disadvantages of the different styles that have been developed and proven over recent years.

To players of experience it will be obvious that systems should be mixed to suit a whole range of requirements, from the individuals available through to the sort of match involved. Ultimately it is the choice of the coach, helped where possible by the senior members of the squad, to send out the right eleven players briefed on the most appropriate system to deal with the particular job in hand.

The accepted similarities between the games of hockey and soccer have led to a new accepted labelling of positions on both fields. These are set out in some detail overleaf. As you will see, the first is the conventional 5–3–2 formation universal in soccer until the advent of the sweeper system in the mid-1960s. The other is 4–3–3, adventurous by modern soccer standards but popular in hockey circles. Although the two systems advocate different individual playing roles, in reality there is little difference between the 5–3–2 and 4–3–3 systems. The game is ultimately influenced by *how* each player keeps his or her position; individual roles can vary even when position on the field remains the same. One system or another, in theory, may make more players available for attacking roles, but in reality it will still depend on how each position is played and which combinations are achieved to decide just which is the more attacking or defensive system. In addition, it should be stressed that there are really no hard and fast rules because the balance of play will always dictate whether a team is spending more time on defence or attack, and all playing systems should be flexible enough to be changed as a game progresses.

The 5–3–2 System

Successful team play is based on a system of simple triangles. These may be formed either by the movement of the ball or the movement of players with the ball. The conventional 5–3–2 system is generally reckoned to be the most economical for players in all areas of the field. However, it is important to understand that for this system to work, all eleven players must play their part both in attack and defence. Usually the 5–3–2 formation is operated in conjunction with zonal marking, where players take responsibility for policing each and every opponent who strays into their designated area of the field. This formation offers the maximum cover and support for the defending team so that once the attack has been broken down and a counter-strike launched, enough players will be on hand to take advantage of the full width of the field. With triangular positioning in operation, the player who wins the ball will always have at least two team-mates to whom he can easily pass.

This system naturally has its drawbacks too, usually when opponents take swift advantage of the space created when one marker hands over his player to a team-mate. The danger here is the creation of a serious work overload for the inside-forwards who are already heavily committed and therefore crucial to the success of this system. It remains the job of the inside-forwards both to win the ball and in so doing to break down attacks, and to make themselves constantly available to receive the ball and provide the springboard for the counter-strike. This system also places considerable onus on the goalkeeper who, on occasion,

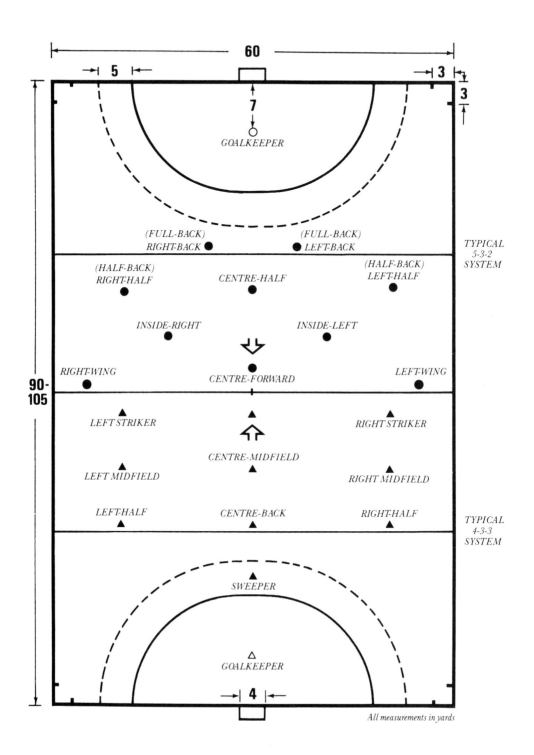

All measurements in yards

will be left with only marginal cover in the final third of the field. In this event, the goalkeeper must remain particularly alert and be prepared to dominate the circle.

The European Styles (4–3–3, 4–2–4, 4–2–3–1)

For many years hockey, like soccer, was dominated by convention and the norm was the 5–3–2 system. However, in recent years coaches have generally adopted a more scientific approach to the game and this has brought about the evolution of new styles of play and a new range of formats which have been adopted to a greater or lesser degree by the world's hockey-playing nations.

Most of these systems make use of a deep-lying defensive player, usually a sweeper, who is given the freedom to plug gaps in the defensive pattern and create a greater depth in the team's play in this area of the field. The sweeper can also be a key player when it comes to launching the counter-attack because often, once in possession, he is in a position to quickly exploit any openings in the attacking line and find one of his own team-mates in space beyond.

Systems like this differ from the conventional 5–3–2 format mainly in the fact that they rely on player-to-player marking rather than zonal cover. Here each player is given responsibility for a specific opponent rather than a particular pocket of the field, and generally players find this an easy way of playing the game and adapt quickly. Their roles are clearly identified and therefore they believe they are becoming more efficient players. In reality, I'm afraid this apparent rigidity makes for the principle flaw in the format because players find it much more difficult to adapt if moves are created that go beyond the constraints of the system. Clearly the sweeper does remain as the last line of defence and, as such, a safety valve, but there is a limit to what he can do to retrieve matters if he is left exposed by an inventive attacking move which penetrates the cover in front of him.

At the end of the day, there are certain vital ingredients that will bring success on the field regardless of what system of play a team adopts. The ability of individual players to interact, interchange and then manipulate opponents and force them into making mistakes will always be the overall recipe for success.

Every successful player will be expected to add the qualities of personal style to the disciplines of the team game. In view of this, therefore, it is not possible to draw up rigid guidelines to cover the particular demands associated with every position on the field. There are, however, a number of basic rules that apply to any player trying to fulfil a particular role, and these can be identified thus:

Sweeper – this role demands a player with good footwork and mobility. The

Fig. 33 Systems of play: The strength of the 5-3-2 system is the amount of triangulation available, while continental systems such as the 4-3-3 give a simpler role definition and produce 'pockets' of players who work together in areas of the field, while keeping one player free to sweep behind the defence.

successful sweeper will be strong in the tackle and a positive and accurate passer of the ball. Equally, he or she will have a fine tactical brain and be a practised reader of the game.

Full-backs – these players should encompass all the skills of the sweeper, plus a generous quota of stamina to enable them to operate over the greater length of the field throughout the duration of the match.

Centre-back – strength in the tackle and the ability to stick close to an opponent at all times are the key qualities for this role. The complete centre-back will usually be a strong physical player prepared to 'mix it a little' when the occasion demands.

Left-half – this position demands all the qualities of the tight defender plus speed because this player will often be called upon to mark the opposition's fastest players.

Right-half – a key position which often provides the springboard for the counter-attack. A quick brain and first-class distribution skills are essential.

Centre-half/Centre-midfield – to steal some soccer parlance, this player is right in the 'engine room'. A strong all-rounder with vision is the best way I can sum up the demands of this job. Suffice it to say that this is not a position for the novice as it is one of the most demanding in the team.

Inside-right/Right-midfield/Inside-left/Left-midfield – close control, stamina, speed and vision are needed here. Generally these are the players who really make things happen. A quick brain to sum up the options and then execute a telling pass – all in the time it takes to blink – are the sort of qualities that can turn a match.

Right-wingers/Right-attack – pace and close control are essential in a player who will spend most of the match trying to get into space beyond the marker and then either produce a telling pass or a cross.

Left-wingers/Left-attack – all the requirements of the right-winger are needed here, plus the particular skill of either wrong-footing an opponent or passing him on the open side using one-handed stick techniques. This is a particularly difficult position to play because it demands much hitting off the wrong foot.

Centre-forwards/Centre-strikers – a glamour position dominated by those special players who can always find the space and the time to get in a shot, no matter how tightly they find themselves marked. Pace and power go without saying, but equally important is the mental ability to anticipate situations and always appear in the right place at the right time.

Goalkeeper – strong physical skills are essential along with mental alertness to maintain concentration even during periods of inactivity. A clear and confident understanding of angles is also important, plus an ability to read the game and help out team-mates with advice and instructions.

Set Pieces

Unlike other team games where the laws are apparently down in tablets of stone never to be revised or tampered with, hockey keeps an open mind about its rules and amendments are constantly being made to ensure that the game keeps pace with change. As the game develops – and particularly in recent years since the revolution of the artificial surface – new restrictions are regularly applied to set pieces. Some of these restrictions are classified as experimental, others permanent, and the job of the players and their coach is to work out systems that enable them to take full advantage of the laws without breaking them.

Free Hits

When you win a free hit it offers the chance to capitalise on possession, and transfer the point of attack as quickly as possible to gain the greatest advantage. The Australian international Ric Charlesworth is recognised as the master of this particular ploy, mainly because of the speed with which he makes up his mind as to where he is going to put the ball and then shoots it beyond the opposition's first defensive wall. Making the most of free hits is an area every team should take the time to work on.

If, on the other hand, the free hit has been awarded against your side, then your objective should be to slow down the progress of the attacking side and to prevent the ball being moved into a more advantageous position. 'Professional conduct', born out of experience, is often the key to successful delaying tactics, buying those few extra seconds which enable the rest of the defence to re-group. Once this has been achieved, the next objective should be to cover in such a way that a ring is thrown around the ball and its passage directed into the area of least danger (usually out towards the sidelines). A typical 'ring' is shown below.

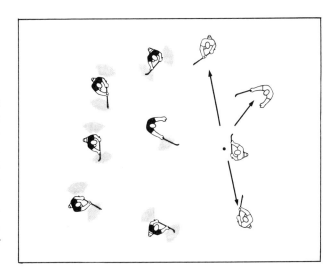

Fig 34 Ringing a free hit: In an ideal situation, the free hit is 'ringed' in such a way that all forward passes can be intercepted, forcing the defender to play a square or backward pass in order to avoid the ring of attackers. Notice that the simple principles of triangulation apply even in ringing the ball, giving depth of cover over the widest possible area.

Push-ins

These should be treated the same way as any free hit, although obviously one half of the field is unavailable. The team in possession will often produce a square or backwards pass and in so doing open up the angles for the receiving player to carve out the advantage.

Long Corners

These are specialised push-ins with the advantage that they are taken close by the area of most danger – the circle. Attacking players within the circle will almost certainly be tightly marked, so the striker of the ball must quickly establish an area of weakness – either a gap in the formation or the reverse side of a particular defender – and hit the ball at it. The gamble here is that a mistake will be made or an opening exploited and the ball will pass through into a goalscoring position.

Defensively, a team should look to create a 'wall' with few flaws and a significant depth of cover. A typical defensive formation is shown below.

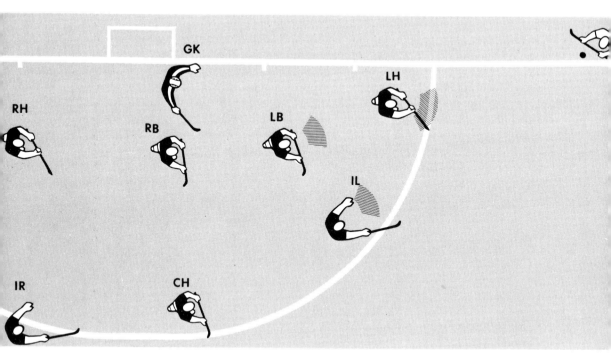

Fig 35 *The Long Corner: Following a similar principle to ringing a free hit, the defence creates a wall of cover, forcing the pass to areas of least danger. The attacking objective will be to play a pass into a scoring position, or force an error by the defence which will concede a penalty corner.*

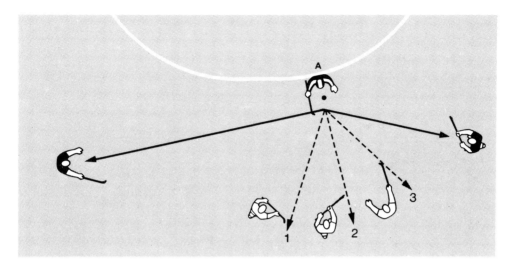

Fig 36 *The sixteen-yard hit.*

The Sixteen-yard Hit

This is generally looked upon as the hockey equivalent of soccer's goal kick. It is awarded in the same way, but should not be set up as a formal exercise. The sixteen-yard hit should always be taken as quickly as possible, the objective being to move the ball immediately to an area of greater advantage. The opposition will always do its best to prevent this happening and often their players will throw a ring around the area in an attempt to prevent the ball being moved. Under these circumstances it is up to defenders to help force a gap and enable the ball to be hit through and hopefully on to a team-mate positioned at the halfway line or beyond. On the other hand, if the attacking side rallies quickly enough and manages to prevent the ball being hit into a safe position, they will retain the advantage and consequently keep up the pressure.

Penalty Corners

The significance of the penalty corner is something that has increased beyond measure over the last decade thanks to a number of significant changes in the laws governing it. Nowadays it amounts virtually to a free shot at goal and although volumes could probably be written about attacking and defensive formations to cope with it, many of these tactics remain vulnerable to the regular changes in the rules of the game.

The objectives of both the attacking and defensive formations at the penalty corner are to secure an advantage, and it has been argued by many of the game's experts that the best way to achieve this is through simplicity. Let's take a look at this set piece from both perspectives.

From the attacker's point of view the prime objective is to create the best

The England penalty corner 'team' line up for their 'free shot' during the 1986 World Cup. The individual roles – Jon Potter pushes out, Sean Kerly stick stops with Richard Dodds and Paul Barber lining up to strike – synchronise to make an efficent goalscoring machine, supported by the secondary rebound tasks of the other forwards. Matches are often won or lost by the precision of the penalty corner routine.

scoring opportunity. Naturally, the more elements introduced into the move the more risk there is of it breaking down, and therefore the ball that is pushed or hit out and then stopped and struck at goal remains the most effective. Nevertheless, depending on the strength of the opposition, variations will be needed from time to time if the attacking side is to capitalise on the enormous advantage that this free hit can offer. The possible options are endless, but a few simple ones are shown below.

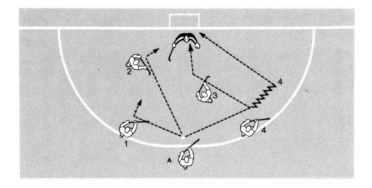

Fig 37 *Attacking alternatives in the penalty corner.*

The many changes in the rules of the game have had their most profound effect on the tactics of players defending the penalty corner. That said, there remain a few simple objectives which, if followed, should improve your chances of successfully preventing the opposition from scoring:

1. If at all possible you should stop the attacking side getting in a shot or goal. If this proves impossible, however, you should concentrate on forcing your opponent to shoot at goal from as far away as possible (ideally the full sixteen yards) and from the narrowest of angles.

2. Rush the opposition and force them to make their plays in haste, thus reducing their chances of executing the move successfully.

3. Anticipate what your opponent is trying to accomplish and in doing so you will improve your chances of making a successful interception or, failing that, persuade the attacking player to change his mind and thereby increase the possibility of the move breaking down.

One of the current rules covering the penalty corner dictates that the striker's first shot must hit the eighteen-inch baseboard at the back of the net to count as a goal. Many goalkeepers have now begun charging corners or lying down on their line to reduce the chances of success. There are some fairly obvious dangers associated with this tactic and the chances of injury are high. In my view, it is a manoeuvre that should be carried out only by goalkeepers who are both properly kitted out and well aware of the risks. It is not a tactic I would advise any coach to persuade a reluctant participant to indulge in.

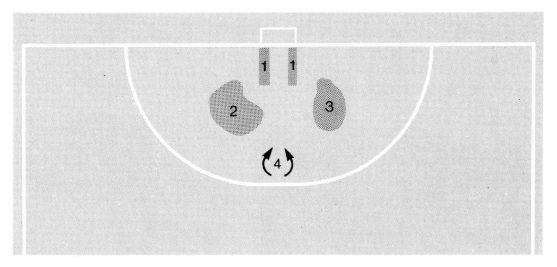

Fig 38 *Primary areas of defence in the penalty corner: Defensive capabilities in the penalty corner are obviously limited, because of the reduced compliment of players. However, the primary areas of defence are highlighted here, and should be discussed by the players concerned. With good teamwork and understanding, the chance of the opponents scoring at a penalty corner can be much reduced.*

Defence of the penalty corner: The Great Britain defence conceded over thirty penalty corners during its Los Angeles Olympic Bronze medal match in 1984. Their opponents Australia only scored from one of these, a defensive record that developed through practice and understanding by all involved. No matter what rule changes are made to the penalty corner, it will always be a key element in the success of a team at any level.

Whatever style of defence is adopted, there remain a number of areas where the goalkeeper is most vulnerable. These areas are highlighted in fig. 38, but to explain a little further they are:

1. The channels beyond the goalkeeper's reach whether he or she is standing up or lying down. Remember, a goalkeeper lying down to cover the left-hand post will inevitably increase the size of the area of danger inside the right-hand post.

2. This is the no man's land in front of the goalkeeper where an attacker might latch onto a through ball to strike or flick at goal from close range.

3. The ball in this area has been played through onto the goalkeeper's reverse or foot side, and the danger will come either from the short range shot or deflection.

4. This is the position in which the spreading goalkeeper is most vulnerable. Often it is the attacker who can keep his cool in the face of the spread-eagled goalkeeper who comes out on top, with a flick over the advancing body to leave the defence paralysed.

Games have been won and lost from the penalty corner and the importance of the move both from the point of view of defence and attack cannot be overstated. Many are the teams who have lost championships and important cup ties as a direct result of a momentary yet costly lapse during one of these set pieces.

The Penalty Stroke

Offences committed within the 'D' and often preventing an attempt on goal are punished by the penalty stroke which amounts to a contest of wits between the striker and goalkeeper at short range. The psychology involved both in taking the stroke and defending it have been the subject of great debate, but in reality the issue is quite simple. The player taking the stroke must attempt to push or flick the ball as hard and as accurately as possible while the 'keeper, through a mixture of highly tuned reflexes and good guesswork, has to try to save it. The use of dummies, false body movements and false messages is not allowed, but if the flick is hard enough and accurate enough there should really be no chance of the goalkeeper making a save.

The four main areas of the goal to aim for are shown in fig. 29. For the goal-keeper, however, the issue is not quite so clear cut. He can either focus his entire attention on the stationary ball and then follow his natural reactions the moment it is flicked, or make a pre-determined guess and commit himself completely, regardless of whether or not it turns out to be entirely the wrong direction. Either way it has to be accepted that when it comes to the penalty stroke, the odds are stacked firmly in favour of the man on strike!

Hockey is a game controlled by two whistles, both in the hands of the umpires, and any one game may be punctuated by fifty or more stoppages, each leading to a set piece and an opportunity for the team in possession to make some progress. When teams are evenly matched these set pieces and the way in which they are handled can often prove to be the only difference between the two sides. In my view, the importance of set-piece skills cannot be exaggerated, and I'm sure that the teams which start taking them as seriously as some of the more conventional aspects of the game will enjoy a significant improvement in their results.

To summarise this chapter then:

• The success or failure of a team is dependent on the efficiency with which individual players arrange themselves into a particular system;

• Free hits in attack should be taken either very quickly or with very precise objectives which are understood by all involved;

• Many games are won or lost by the efficiency of the attacking and defensive formations at set pieces;

• Only by precise objectives being well defined will any individual member be able to fulfill his or her role in any given situation.

COACHING AND TRAINING

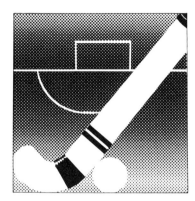

Successful hockey, like all sporting activities, demands a level of commitment. It is no good merely turning up on the day and expecting to be able to turn in a world class performance. Behind each move and technique lie many hours of training, practice, thought and discussion. It follows, therefore, that as the standard of competition improves, the hours spent on the practice field become all the more important. Throughout this book I have been at pains to stress the fact that hockey is a simple game. However, it is equally important to understand that it is also a game that demands match fitness at all times. By match fitness, I don't merely mean fitness of a physical kind. In this instance I'm referring more to a mental sharpness which stems from a feeling of well-being in a player who has worked hard to be in tip-top condition on match day.

The majority of players reading this book will be doing so because they want to improve their play and are therefore prepared to dedicate more of their time to the game. Having said that, however, it is important to set realistic targets geared to the amount of time you have available and the standard of hockey you wish to achieve. Training and practice are essential in any sport and in hockey there are a number of specific exercises that can be included in any schedule.

For anyone overweight or generally out of condition, a little regular exercise of any nature will always improve performance on the field of play but in reality, jogging is of little real value to the hockey player except as a way of improving general aerobic capacity. At the highest level an international player will cover anything up to five miles during the course of a game, but it doesn't follow that by embarking on a series of five-mile training runs a player would do anything to improve his or her game. Indeed it has been shown that this sort of activity can have a negative effect.

Hockey involves an enormous amount of sprinting, turning, stopping, starting and back peddling, so any physical training programme should certainly incorporate all these movements. Time should also be spent running in the back bent position unique to hockey and which I have described in Chapter 1.

Few players enjoy the experience of 'hitting the wall' during pure physical training, therefore coaches should be sure to include an element of fun in all their training schedules. This will help give players the incentive to push harder and in so doing they will be improving their physical shape still further.

I have already isolated the skills of hockey during earlier chapters, and these movements can all be practised alone. This I would recommend particularly for novice players because it enables them to master the various elements of the game at their own speed, identifying and correcting any weaknesses that become apparent. Once happy with a basic style, players should progress to working on their skills in groups and, wherever possible, simulating match conditions. Having already spoken about the problems of those players who look superb on the training field and then seem to disappear in a real match, I cannot over-emphasise the need for coaches to constantly expose their players to decision-making. This will help develop that all-important instinct for being in the right place at the right time. Even when players are forced to practise alone, it is still possible to create self-imposed restrictions that can lead to the sort of movements and actions likely to occur in a real game.

Flexibility is another key to producing better players at any level of the game. It follows that the more formal and routine the practice sessions, the more rigid the style of the player they produce. Coaches are often seen pulling their hair out because a particular player is always rigid and predictable in both style and tactics. In more cases than not, that same coach will be largely responsible for the unadventurous approach of his team because of his own adherence to regimented activities in training.

The multi-faceted roles of the coach will be discussed later, but for the moment it is sufficient to say that every team with a hunger for success should have one at the helm. An experienced outside viewpoint will always help when it comes to improving a team's overall play and creating the all-important balance necessary for consistency. Players of every standard will benefit from the influence of a coach and it doesn't follow that experienced players outgrow them.

There are a number of other factors which influence a player's performance and the psychological element is one which should never be overlooked. Mental fitness is every bit as important as physical fitness, both in the case of the individual and the team, and I doubt whether any amount of practice or training could help a team achieve consistent success unless their attitude was also psychologically right.

Having said all this, I must go on to stress the most important element of all and that is enjoyment! The whole point of this book is to help improve playing standards, and by improving standards it should follow that the level of enjoyment is improved too. Essentially sport is played for social reasons, to produce a fitter, healthier human being, and when a player loses sight of this – regardless of the standard of play achieved – he has lost the point of sport altogether.

Training

Muscle strength and stamina are both important to the hockey player, whether it is a case of getting fit enough to last a game, or developing the endurance to get through the pressures of a tournament involving a number of games over a short period of time. However, it should also be stressed that success in the game is not determined solely on the grounds of physical strength.

Aerobic capacity – the ability to take in and effectively use oxygen – can be improved by endurance training. A wide range of these exercises has been well documented and the *fartlek*, or interval training, is particularly useful for the hockey player. This activity involves regular changes of pace (walk – jog – sprint – flat-out) and also changes of direction. It mirrors to some extent the movements of an outfield player during the game itself. Some players find it enjoyable to take part in repetition runs over longer distances (800 – 600 – 400 metres etc). This is not something everyone would describe as fun, but each to his own. Whatever style or variety of styles you choose to adopt, you would be well advised to borrow a book from the local library or consult a coach before devising a programme.

I'm including in this chapter a few exercises that work on aerobic capacity and enable the player to practise a variety of skills at the same time. This is by far the best way to get fit for hockey, but unfortunately not always practicable.

Aerobic capacity is directly related to the frequency of training and the player who, for whatever reason, takes a few weeks off will inevitably find himself 'short of wind' on returning to training. It is also common for performance to deteriorate during the early stages of training and this is because the body requires time to adjust to the demands of physical overload. It is important not to become disheartened at this stage; coaches should be aware of the problem and be prepared to offer extra encouragement to the player who unrealistically expects his fitness to improve overnight just because he has started to train.

As aerobic capacity improves, players should begin improving their agility, by means of regular stretching exercises, and should work to increase their strength in relation to the specific demands of the game. Strength training should pay particular attention to the wrists and forearms, the lower back and, in particular, the hamstrings, which should be worked with the body in the bent or crouched position. Strength is improved by working each particular group of muscles against an overload. This load should be increased periodically as physical strength improves.

The use of weights, multi-station units and combinations of pulleys and springs has been well publicised and they are becoming more and more available both in health clubs and at sports centres. However, for those unable to gain access to them there are a variety of other methods of strength training that require little more than your own body weight. These include body resistance exercises such as press-ups and sit-ups; isometric training where muscular contractions are performed regularly against an immovable resistance such as a wall; and plyometrics or bounding where a muscle is stretched to its full limit followed by a rapid contraction. Where possible, these sessions should also include work on some of the more physical skills, such as flicking or hitting for example.

Advice should always be taken on the type and intensity of an individual programme because different numbers of repetitions (the number of times a particular exercise is performed without stopping) will produce different effects. Generally the formula for strength training shows that muscular endurance is achieved by completing a large number of repetitions each with low resistances, while muscular strength is achieved against large loads or resistances with fewer repetitions. The balance between muscular strength and endurance is fine and must be carefully tailored to suit the needs of the individual.

Some forms of weights are particularly beneficial to hockey players and an example that springs immediately to mind is 'wrist rolling', using either a special wrist rolling machine or a brick attached to a broom handle! The moral is that anyone can train, whatever the availability of equipment. All it takes is a little thought and imagination.

It is generally agreed that two or three exercise sessions a week are sufficient to produce significant gains in strength and stamina. However, as I stressed at the outset, this is all determined by your own aspirations. An Olympic hockey player would probably talk in terms of twelve to twenty exercise sessions per week built into a programme that would also include specialised practice and between two and three full-scale games. The sacrifices involved in reaching Olympic standard are enormous and many of those who aspire to this level of competition fall by the wayside because of other commitments long before they achieve their full potential. The satisfaction of having played in the Olympic Games, however, is a more than ample reward for all the pain and torment on the way there.

Simple Strength Training Exercises

SIT-UPS – Sit on floor or an inclined bench with the feet flat and the knees bent, and your hands behind your neck. Pull yourself up until your elbows touch your knees and then lower down until your elbows are flat on the floor. Repeat, moving your right elbow to your left knee, then your left elbow to your right knee and finally back to both elbows to both knees.

PRESS-UPS – Take up the front support position with your back straight and lower yourself until your nose is touching the floor and then push up quickly. If possible try to make the exercise more dynamic by clapping your hands as you push-up.

BACK RAISES – Lie flat on the floor with arms and legs spread-eagled, then lift arms, legs and head as high off the floor as possible.

SEATED LEVERS – Sitting on the floor, straighten your arms, then raise your legs off the floor.

SQUAT JUMPS – Crouch down and touch the floor and then jump as high as possible throwing the arms into the air, land and return to the squat position.

Simple Plyometric (Bounding) Exercises

HURDLE SPRINGS – From the front simply make repeated jumps over an object, keeping the feet together and flexing the knees through as large an angle as possible. Then stand side on to the hurdle and repeat the exercise.

BOX JUMP (A couple of boxes or a low wall are needed for this) – Place a pair of boxes about a metre apart and keeping the feet together, jump from box to floor to box repeatedly.

These are just a few examples of the many training exercises that have been devised over the years. Your coach or your local leisure centre should have additional and more specific information.

Some sharp-eyed physical educationalists will notice that I have omitted speed work from the training guide. This is a deliberate move for which I offer no apology. In my view this is one area in particular where many players and coaches seem to be steered by convention and fail to take into account the basic requirements of hockey. For the majority, the development of speed should be related to practices rather than training because the type of running involved – with backs crouched, knees bent or even just running with a stick in your hands while twisting and weaving – is difficult to execute without a ball. And it should also be remembered that in hockey there is always a skill to complete, be it shooting at goal, putting in a tackle or manoeuvring into a correct position in relation to your opponent.

However, the coach, as motivator of the squad, should carefully monitor his players for speed during practice sessions and push them to new limits.

Practising and Coaching

Many players practise badly and yet are surprised when their match performance is disappointing. The amount of time spent on practice, the type of practice performed and the attitude taken during practice will inevitably be directly related to match performance. Few people can just go out on the day and play to their full potential.

In hockey, as with any sport, there is a progression from the initial learning of the basic skills up to the point where they become second nature, even under the greatest match-day pressure. Unfortunately, even at the highest level, players often find themselves forced to practise their skills in isolation. While this enables them to perfect the technical skills involved in a particular movement, it doesn't prepare them for the problems associated with trying to achieve the same levels of expertise in the heat of battle.

Initially a skill or movement must be broken down into its fundamentals, and then problems of technique identified and eliminated. Once this has been achieved, a player should be encouraged to develop confidence in his or her ability to use it in real circumstances and this is the point at which group practice should start. The coach must take responsibility for creating a wide range of match-like situations. Far too many practices are carried out in stationary or near-stationary positions – probably the one situation you are never likely to find yourself in under match conditions.

Hockey is a fast-moving game and the players and the ball are rarely stationary. What is more, the ball is carried over a wide variety of angles and at different heights and speeds. Practices should take this into account and the aim should be to make them as interesting and realistic to the player as possible. They should always be specific to a particular skill and, where possible, have a target or objective, whether goalscoring, executing a successful tackle, or completing a particular exercise in a set time. These restrictions, either self-imposed or organised by a coach, are of vital importance if improvement is to be maintained.

Practices should always be assessed and evaluated both during and after the exercise so that weaknesses can be identified and corrected and new ideas discussed. Handled in the right spirit and with the contribution of everyone involved, critical analysis can prove a positive help to any side because it serves to stimulate team spirit and maintain the interest and competitive edge of each of the players.

The coach should see himself as chairman of a committee, willing and able to take on board a wide diversity of opinion. Even with children it is important not to introduce rigid routines and to take care to introduce as many 'real' match situations into practices as possible. And when devising practices – whether for oneself, a small group of players or for a team – they should be introduced broadly along the development line below. Naturally, the point at which a player joins the line will depend very much on his experience, a newcomer obviously starting at point one, a reasonable club player at points two or three and a top-class performer at points four or five. Of course there will be occasions when an opportunity arises to use a new skill in a match before all these stages have been completed. This opportunity should never be ignored, but if you try it and it doesn't quite come off, this doesn't mean that you've failed. Your chances of success will improve when all stages have been completed.

Primary objectives of the coach

1	2	3	4	5	6	7	8	9	10
BASIC SKILL IN ISOLATION		SKILL UNDER RESTRICTION		SKILL IN SMALL-SIDED SITUATION		SKILL IN SMALL-SIDED SITUATION WITH LIMITATIONS IMPOSED		SKILL IMPLEMENTED IN FULL MATCH-PLAY SITUATION	

I've already stressed the importance of that outside critical eye in spotting weaknesses and offering advice, and because it follows that no one particular method can be judged absolutely correct, the coach must be prepared to be flexible in thought and able to offer suggestions that are adaptations or compromises. Sometimes this might involve a little inventiveness or imagination. (I remember one story of a leading Dutch coach who, having found it very difficult to get a group of young children to allow the stick to turn in their right hand, slid empty toilet roll tubes onto the handle and let the youngsters grip this to get a feel for the turning stick with their right hands stationary.)

I have tried to define my view of the role of the coach below, with emphasis on the upper end of the table for those dealing with younger or inexperienced players and on the lower end for all those operating at the higher level. All of these duties, however, are the responsibility of the good coach and he should be able to give advice and help in relation to age and ability in each department.

Table to show the objectives of the coach

- Teaching, improving and correcting basic skills
- Combining individual activity into group work
- Making isolated skills work in match-like situations
- Devising and implementing a team strategy and outlining individual roles
- Constructing practices that develop the team strategy and set pieces
- Planning and monitoring the physical development of the team
- Motivating the players to perform above themselves
- Communicating with the team to produce a more effective unit

To state the obvious, the coach is responsible for the development of the players under his control and sometimes improvements do take time, so patience is an essential quality. The good coach is not afraid to learn from his mistakes and is constantly streamlining practices and revising his attitude to the game, seeking new ideas and enthusiastically putting them into operation. Predetermined views or tunnel vision will lead to little team or individual success, and the pleasure of the game will quickly be lost as lines of communication are severed and team members become dissatisfied. Coaches need also to look to themselves for development alongside the team they are responsible for. This way individuals, teams and the coaches themselves will derive maximum success and enjoyment from the game.

Individual Practices

Here are just a few practices for the individual to work on when mastering the basic skills contained in the preceding chapters. The intention is to create self-imposed pressures on each of the skills in an effort to create the match-day realism that I have talked about. Practised properly, it is hoped most players will learn to pull off the same manoeuvre under the most severe pressure during a game.

THE DRIBBLE

Stop dribble: Find an area, such as a tennis court, which has several lines on it, or alternatively an area of paving slabs. Dribble with the ball in front until you come to a line and then stop the ball dead. Then set off at speed at forty five degrees to the line until you reach the next line or obstruction and repeat the stop. Concentrate on stopping the ball dead, keeping your head up to improve your scanning and then accelerating sharply away from the dead ball position. Constantly change direction across the complete range, left to right and forwards and back.

Indian dribble: Scatter at random several cones and bricks over a limited area. Dribble the ball around for five seconds, walking for five seconds and then jogging for a further five and follow with five seconds at full speed. Mark some of the cones and bricks and then whenever you pass one of these discipline yourself to change your direction by ninety degrees either to the left or the right, without straying outside the limits of the area.

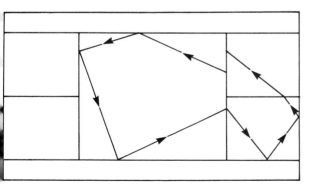

Fig 39 *Practising the stop dribble*

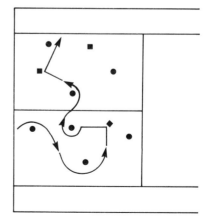

Fig 40 *Practising the Indian dribble*

THE PUSH

This is one practice that can be applied to all types of pushing exercises. The speed with which the ball is brought into position and the power and accuracy of the push are the key factors. Stand several plastic bottles at random and three or four cones or bricks at some distance away, with balls behind a starting line. Run back and collect a ball, dribble through the cones or bricks, then finish the exercise by pushing to the left if you pass to the right of the last obstacle and to the right if you leave it to your left. The test is to see how many balls it takes you to knock down all the bottles.

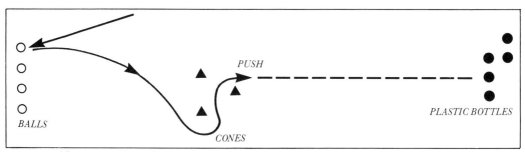

Fig 41 *Practising the push*

STOPPING THE BALL

This is a skill often practised with a partner or in a group, but it can also be practised to great effect on your own by switching the hockey ball for something of a similar size but with more bounce. A tennis ball will do, but a hard rubber ball is even better. The exercise simply involves striking the ball against the corner of a wall at varying speeds and heights. I've even heard of an Australian Olympic player who used to spend hours practising this particular technique using a golf ball – which would naturally prove extremely difficult to control in this exercise.

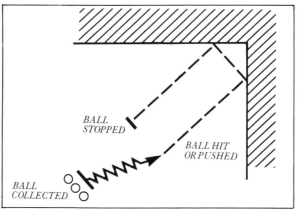

Fig 42 *Practising stopping the ball*

THE HIT

Targets such as plastic bottles or cones are ideal and the practice described for the push works equally well for the hit. Inevitably the time allowed should be the conditioning factor and therefore time limits should be self-imposed. A good player, for example, should hope to complete eight successful strikes in thirty seconds when running with the ball. It is important that the player concentrates on the quality of the hit, with accuracy being the vital factor.

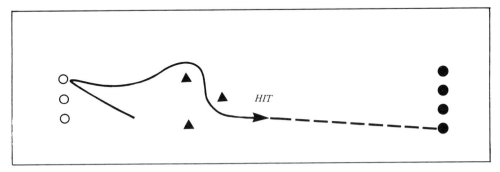

Fig 43 *Practising the hit*

THE FLICK

Mark a wall into zones using tape or chalk. The object is to flick the ball into each zone in turn, moving onto the zone above only after success with the one below. The important element here is to practise collecting the ball and quickly position-ing the feet, head and body for the flick. You should either move to collect the new ball or, better still, collect the rebound off the wall from the last flick. You will therefore be practising stopping the ball and getting it into position for the flick, and thus preparing yourself for a real-match situation. The skill can be further refined simply by restricting the size of the zones or increasing your distance from the wall. This is also an exercise which lends itself to time limits.

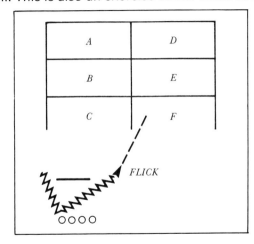

Fig 44 *Practising the flick*

BEATING AN OPPONENT

The role of mental imagery will be discussed after these practices but it plays a key role in creating match-like situations, using a combination of obstacles and imagination. By navigating several obstacles, the physical movements of swerving, dodging and moving the ball can be practised. Having received the ball or collected it from behind, the objective is to move the ball over as large a distance to the side as possible while retaining complete control, then cut back in behind the obstacles, thus simulating the skill of cutting your opponent out of the game. The positions and orders of the obstacles will depend very much on your imagination, but you should keep a steady pace until you reach the 'opponent', then you should accelerate around and beyond him.

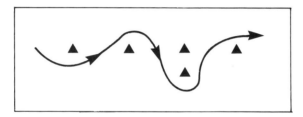

Fig 45 *Practising beating an opponent*

TACKLING

This is obviously the most difficult skill to practise in isolation and competitive practice with team mates is always preferable. However, I found the answer in part while talking to an Indian Olympic player who found the jab tackle by far the most pleasurable way to remove troublesome daisies from his lawn! As I have already said, imagination and improvisation are the keys to success in this game.

GOALKEEPING

Goalkeeping practices usually involve several players and can be fully included in the group activities described later. Personally I'm particularly keen on practising body balance and control, and one of the simple practices I strongly recommend involves the use of a corner of a squash court or similar structure. Use a variety of balls: table tennis balls, squash balls, tennis balls and hard bouncy rubber balls. Play each in turn into the corner and then see how long you can keep a rally going using your legs and feet but restricting the ball to one bounce, then no bounces at all as you progress. The object of the exercise is to make the maximum use of legs and feet.

GOALSCORING

The art of goalscoring was described earlier as the ability to use a variety of shots from different angles and at varying speeds. In the absence of other players to serve the shooter, the player must receive the ball off a wall or bench, run to collect it on the rebound, then shoot, changing the angles between each shot. This type of practice is particularly demanding and combines shooting skills with the rigours of physical training. It involves sprints with and without the ball, stops and turns. The balls can be adjusted to accommodate flicks from a closer range, slap hits and pushes into the corner while on the run. You should also, of course, reverse the practice by moving the goal position.

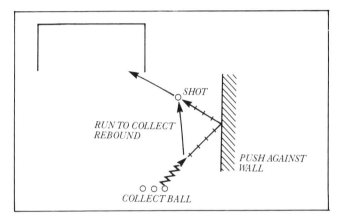

Fig 46 Practising goalscoring

TEAM AND GROUP PLAY/SYSTEMS AND SET PIECES

In these chapters the players are being called upon to use a combination of separate skills to complete their objectives. In practice, a variety of restrictions can be imposed to make each exercise more game-like. The amount of time available, the number of passes made and the presence of passive or active opponents will all be used in the development of combined activity, so the following exercises are geared to several players practising together.

Wall-Passes – Pushing – Hitting – Flicking: Player A on the outside passes the ball to player B in the centre of a 10-metre circle. Player B wall-passes the ball to another player not adjacent to the player who made the initial pass. The player in the middle may not wall-pass the ball in the same direction more than three consecutive times. This practice can be adapted for a number of skills or, even better, a combination of skills, as long as the players involved are of the same standard. With the ball constantly coming back to the man in the middle, who moves towards the ball to receive it, the movement of the body and feet, combined with continual scanning, ensure that this is a tiring but particularly constructive exercise.

Fig 47 wall passing

Group activities: Even the youngest player will soon be able to cope with small game-like activities. Starting with 'piggy in the middle', move from two-versus-one to three-against-two and so on. It is this simple overloading principle that is the basis for a large number of more successful group practices. Whether it is three attackers versus two defenders or one defender and a goalkeeper, all the combined skills of stopping, pushing, flicking and shooting at goal can be successfully incorporated into one overload exercise.

This should prove the basis of most coached exercises where the number of participating players is low and the level of activity high and specific. Introducing extra demands like only two touches and pushing the ball only, or restricting the exercise to reverse side passes, helps introduce more pressure to the situation.

Although I have decided to include a couple of brief examples, it is very much the imagination of the coach related to the requirements of the players involved in the practice session which will make these exercises useful, rewarding and above all enjoyable.

Quick break attack: Three players start with the ball on the halfway line and the coach blows a whistle and starts his watch. The players might, for example, be given twenty seconds to pass the one defender and shoot at goal. Should the ball rebound off the goalkeeper, they may continue to play and score before the whistle stops the action. Obviously the number of defenders/attackers can be varied and so can the time span.

Sharp shooting: Here the shooter starts just outside the twenty-five with a semi-passive defender marking him. The other forwards in turn carry the ball and pass to the shooter who rounds his opponents and shoots, following in for the rebound if necessary. The ball can be played on by the attacker until either a goal is scored or the goalkeeper clears the circle. The forward then returns to the twenty-five to combine with a different forward for the next shot. On completion of the set, the forwards rotate to give another forward the shooting role.

The number of variations on these themes are limitless, so each exercise must have a clearly defined objective as well as clearly understood targets that are both realistic and achievable. A player should be worked hard, but never into the ground.

CONCLUSION

A player's ability to train and practise effectively and to improve his standard of play has a considerable amount to do with mental attitude. To play above themselves in the big match, even the most seasoned players have to put themselves through a mental building exercise where in their minds they play the perfect game with all the skills intact and their ambitions realised. At one time this attitude might have been dismissed as day-dreaming but nowadays the top coaches consider it to be a fundamental building block for a successful match performance. The belief is that if the player cannot visualise success in his own mind, then he will not achieve that desired level of achievement in the pressurised environment of the game itself.

I firmly believe that a lot of my own success can be attributted to this simple factor. I can at all times clearly picture in my own mind a series of changes of movement which will develop a variation on a technique and thereby create an improved performance. This process of mental imagery is a vital factor in any learning process. It is only when you can visualise yourself successfully completing a skill – with the individual components broken down and understood – that you will understand the skill's requirements and be able to analyse your weak points and rectify them.

At every level – from school to Olympic standard – we play this game of hockey because we enjoy it and because we give enjoyment to others. Sometimes players may lose sight of this, due to the pressures of success or failure. The game will only develop – and you with it – if you keep this fact firmly in sight. Keep practising!

David Whittaker, the England and Great Britain coach, talks to the author during a half-time break in the European Cup (Moscow 1987).

HOCKEY RECORDS

MEN'S HOCKEY

OLYMPIC GAMES   *Winners*
1948	(London)	India
1952	(Helsinki)	India
1956	(Melbourne)	India
1960	(Rome)	Pakistan
1964	(Tokyo)	India
1968	(Mexico)	Pakistan
1972	(Munich)	Germany
1976	(Montreal)	New Zealand
1980	(Moscow)	India
1984	(Los Angeles)	Pakistan

WORLD CUP
1971	(Barcelona)	Pakistan
1973	(Amsterdam)	Netherlands
1975	(Kuala Lumpur)	India
1978	(Buenos Aires)	Pakistan
1982	(Bombay)	Pakistan
1986	(London)	Australia

ASIAN GAMES
1958	(Tokyo)	Pakistan
1962	(Djakarta)	Pakistan
1966	(Bangkok)	India
1970	(Bangkok)	Pakistan

1974	(Teheran)	Pakistan
1978	(Bangkok)	Pakistan
1982	(New Delhi)	Pakistan
1986	(Seoul)	Korea

EUROPEAN CUP
1970	(Brussels)	Germany
1974	(Madrid)	Spain
1978	(Hanover)	Germany
1983	(Amsterdam)	Netherlands
1987	(Moscow)	Netherlands

PAN-AMERICAN GAMES
1967	(Winnipeg)	Argentina
1971	(Cali)	Argentina
1975	(Mexico City)	Argentina
1979	(San Juan)	Argentina
1983	(Caracas)	Canada
1987	(Indianapolis)	Canada

INTER-CONTINENTAL CUP
1977	(Rome)	Poland
1981	(Kuala Lumpur)	USSR
1985	(Barcelona)	Spain

WORLD CUP

FINAL POSITIONS

TEAM	1971	1973	1975	1978	1982	1986
Pakistan	1	4	2	1	1	11
W. Germany	5	3	3	4	2	3
India	3	2	1	6	5	12
Netherlands	6	1	9	2	4	7
Australia	8	—	5	3	3	1
U.S.S.R.	—	—	*ne*	*ne*	6	4
Spain	2	5	8	5	11	5
New Zealand	—	7	7	*ne*	7	9
England	—	6	6	7	9	2
Malaysia	—	11	4	10	10	(15)
Poland	—	—	10	9	8	8

Argentina	10	9	11	8	12	6
Ireland	—	—	—	12	(13)	(13)
Belgium	—	8	—	14	(14)	(16)
Kenya	4	12	—	—	*with*	(14)
Wales	—	—	—	—	(15)	*dnq*
Japan	9	10	—	—	(16)	(17)
France	7	—	—	—	(17)	*dnq*
Canada	—	—	—	11	(18)	10
Ghana	—	—	12	—	—	*ne*
Singapore	—	—	—	—	(19)	*dnq*
Zimbabwe	—	—	—	—	(20)	(19)
Italy	—	—	—	13	(21)	*dnq*
S. Korea	—	—	—	—	—	— (18)

ne did not enter   *with* withdrew   ( ) Intercontinental Cup position   *dnq* did not qualify

INTER-CONTINENTAL CUP

FINAL POSITIONS

TEAM	1977	1981	1985
Argentina	(WC8)	(WC12)	5-Q
Belgium	4-Q	5	9
Canada	5-Q	9	4-Q
France	7	8	*dnq*
Ghana	10	—	*dnq*
India	(WC6)	(WC5)	(WC12)
Ireland	2-Q	4	6
Italy	6-Q	12	*dnq*
Japan	8	7	10
Kenya	9	—	7
Korea	—	—	11
Malaysia	(WC10)	2-Q	8
Mexico	12	—	*with*
Netherlands	(WC2)	(WC4)	(WC7)
Nigeria	11	—	*dnq*
New Zealand	—	3-Q	2-Q
Poland	1-Q	(WC8)	3-Q
Scotland	—	—	*dnq*
Singapore	—	10	*ne*
Spain	(WC5)	(WC11)	1-Q
U.S.A.	—	—	—
U.S.S.R.	3-Q	1-Q	(WC4)
Wales	—	6	*dnq*
Zimbabwe	—	11	121

Q Qualified World Cup (WC) World Cup Position *dnq* did not qualify *ne* did not enter *with* withdrew

EUROPEAN CUP

FINAL POSITIONS

TEAM	1970	1974	1978	1983	1987
Austria	11	15	*dnq*	11	*dnq*
Belgium	5	10	*dnq*	8	10
C.S.S.R.	10	9	10	*dnq*	*ne*
Denmark	18	14	*dnq*	*dnq*	*ne*
England	6	4	3	5	2
Finland	16	18	*dnq*	*ne*	*dnq*
France	4	6	7	6	11
Germany	1	2	1	3	3
Gibraltar	*ne*	*ne*	12	*dnq*	*ne*
Ireland	9	11	8	10	6
Italy	13	12	*dnq*	*dnq*	9
Hungary	17	*ne*	*ne*	*ne*	*ne*
Malta	19	—	*ne*	*ne*	*ne*
Poland	7	5	5	9	5
Portugal	*ne*	16	—	*dnq*	*dnq*
Netherlands	2	3	2	1	1
Scotland	15	7	11	7	8
Sweden	—	—	*dnq*	*dnq*	—
Switzerland	8	17	*dnq*	*dnq*	*dnq*
Spain	3	1	4	4	7
U.S.S.R.	14	*ne*	9	2	4
Wales	12	8	6	12	12
Yugoslavia	*ne*	13	*dnq*	*dnq*	*dnq*

ne did not enter   *dnq* did not quality

Record score: Spain 13 - 0 v Malta 21.9.70

CHAMPIONS TROPHY

FINAL POSITIONS

TEAM	1978	1980	1981	1982	1983	1984	1985	1986	1987
Australia	2	3	2	2	1	1	1	2	3
Germany	—	2	3	5	3	*with*	3	1	1
Great Britain	3	7	6*E*	—	*dnq*	3	2	4	4
India	—	5	—	3	4	*with*	6	5	—
Netherlands	—	4	1	1	5	4	5	6	2
New Zealand	4	—	—	—	6	5	—	—	—
Pakistan	1	1	4	4	2	2	4	3	7
Spain	5	6	5	*dnq*	*dnq*	6	1st Res.	1st Res.	6
Argentina	—	—	—	—	—	—	—	—	5
U.S.S.R.	—	—	—	6	—	—	—	—	8

with withdrew   *E* England   *dnq* did not qualify

ASIAN GAMES

FINAL POSITIONS

TEAM	1958	1962	1966	1970	1974	1978	1982	1986
Bangladesh	—	—	—	—	—	6	9	7
Brunei	—	—	—	—	—	—	—	—
China	—	—	—	—	—	—	—	—
Hong Kong	—	7	7	7	—	5	7	6
India	2	2	1	2	2	2	2	3
Indonesia	—	5	—	—	—	—	—	—
Iran	—	—	—	—	6	—	—	—
Japan	5	4	3	3	4	4	4	5
Malaysia	4	3	4	4	3	3	3	4
Oman	—	—	—	—	—	—	7	8
Pakistan	1	1	2	1	1	1	1	2
Singapore	—	9	—	5	—	—	—	—
S. Korea	3	6	6	—	—	—	5	1
Sri Lanka	—	8	5	6	5	7	—	—
Thailand	—	—	7	8	—	8	—	9

WOMEN'S HOCKEY

OLYMPIC GAMES		*Winners*
1980	(Moscow)	Zimbabwe
1984	(Los Angeles)	Netherlands

WORLD CHAMPIONSHIP (I.F.W.H.A.)		
1971	(Auckland)	Netherlands
1975	(Edinburgh)	England
1979	(Vancouver)	Netherlands
1983	(Kuala Lumpur)	Netherlands

WORLD CUP (F.I.H.)		
1974	(Mandelieu)	Netherlands
1976	(Berlin)	Germany
1978	(Madrid)	Netherlands
1981	(Buenos Aires)	Germany
1983	(Kuala Lumpur)	Netherlands
1986	(Amstelveen)	Netherlands

EUROPEAN CUP		
1984	(Lille)	Netherlands
1988	(London)	Netherlands

PAN-AMERICAN GAMES		
1987	(Indianapolis)	Argentina

INTER-CONTINENTAL CUP		
1983	(Kuala Lumpur)	Ireland
1985	(Buenos Aires)	U.S.S.R.

Hockey records courtesy of Pat Rowley